STUDIES IN ECONOMIC AND SOCIAL HISTORY

This series, specially commissioned by the Economic History Society, provides a guide to the current interpretations of the key themes of economic and social history in which advances have recently been made or in which there has been significant debate.

Originally entitled 'Studies in Economic History', in 1974 the series had its scope extended to include topics in social history, and the new series title, 'Studies in Economic and Social History', signalises this development.

The series gives readers access to the best work done, helps them to draw their own conclusions in major fields of study, and by means of the critical bibliography in each book guides them in the selection of further reading. The aim is to provide a springboard to further work rather than a set of pre-packaged conclusions or short-cuts.

ECONOMIC HISTORY SOCIETY

The Economic History Society, which numbers over 3000 members, publishes the *Economic History Review* four times a year (free to members) and holds an annual conference. Enquiries about membership should be addressed to the Assistant Secretary, Economic History Society, Peterhouse, Cambridge. Full-time students may join at special rates.

STUDIES IN ECONOMIC AND SOCIAL HISTORY

Edited for the Economic History Society by T. C. Smout

PUBLISHED

OTHER TITLES ARE IN PREPARATION

The Aristocracy of Labour in Nineteenth-Century Britain, c.1850 – 1900

Prepared for
The Economic History Society by

ROBERT GRAY

Lecturer in Social History
Portsmouth Polytechnic

M

First published 1981 by
THE MACMILLAN PRESS LTD
London and Basingstoke
Associated companies in Delhi Dublin
Hong Kong Johannesburg Lagos Melbourne
New York Singapore and Tokyo

ISBN 0 333 25330 2

Typeset by Datakey Typesetters (Kent) Ltd
Printed in Hong Kong

Contents

Note on References

References in the text within square brackets relate to the items in the Bibliography, followed, where necessary, by the page numbers in italics, for example [Thompson, 1978, *70*]. Other references in the text, numbered consecutively throughout the book, relate to annotations of the text or to sources not given in the Bibliography, and are itemised in the Notes and References section.

Editor's Preface

SINCE 1968, when the Economic History Society and Macmillan published the first of the 'Studies in Economic and Social History', the series has established itself as a major teaching tool in universities, colleges and schools, and as a familiar landmark in serious bookshops throughout the country. A great deal of the credit for this must go to the wise leadership of its first editor, Professor M. W. Flinn, who retired at the end of 1977. The books tend to be bigger now than they were originally, and inevitably more expensive; but they have continued to provide information in modest compass at a reasonable price by the standards of modern academic publications.

There is no intention of departing from the principles of the first decade. Each book aims to survey findings and discussion in an important field of economic or social history that has been the subject of recent lively debate. It is meant as an introduction for readers who are not themselves professional researchers but who want to know what the discussion is all about — students, teachers and others generally interested in the subject. The authors, rather than either taking a strongly partisan line or suppressing their own critical faculties, set out the arguments and the problems as fairly as they can, and attempt a critical summary and explanation of them from their own judgement. The discipline now embraces so wide a field in the study of the human past that it would be inappropriate for each book to follow an identical plan, but all volumes will normally contain an extensive descriptive bibliography.

The series is not meant to provide all the answers but to help readers to see the problems clearly enough to form their own conclusions. We shall never agree in history, but the discipline will be well served if we know what we are disagreeing about, and why.

T. C. SMOUT

University of St Andrew's   *Editor*

7

1 Introduction

> The working man belonging to the upper class of his order is a member of the aristocracy of the working classes. He is a man of some culture, is well read in political and social history .... His self respect is also well developed (*The Reformer*, 5 November 1870).

THUS George Potter, prominent trade unionist and radical journalist. Similar phrases are scattered through contemporary accounts of the working class in the third quarter of the nineteenth century, emphasising the role of an 'aristocracy of the working classes' distinguished from other workers by their way of life, values and attitudes, as much as by a superior economic position. They were often seen as a moderating influence on the politics of popular protest, contributing to the mid-century disintegration of mass movements such as Chartism. Historians following the lines of enquiry suggested by this contemporary analysis have adopted the term 'labour aristocracy' to indicate such groupings within the working class. How valid are these attempts to identify a distinct upper stratum? And how did divisions within the working class affect the militancy and class consciousness of the labour movement in the decades after 1850? Studies of the labour aristocracy continue to provoke a lively debate around these problems.

Definitions of the labour aristocracy vary, but the use of the term is generally directed to attempts to understand what was happening in the world of industrial labour in the years after about 1850, and how this affected attitudes and organisations. This can be seen as one way of approaching broader problems in the historical analysis of social class. Historians concerned with these problems generally consider classes to be basic elements in the structure of society, defined by unequal relationships of wealth

8

and power; the way that classes relate to each other and cohere as social groups shapes the development of society. Marxism, viewing inequalities in terms of a theory of the exploitation of wage-labour by capital and emphasising class struggle as a fundamental feature of capitalist society, has been a powerful influence in this field of study; but the concern with inequalities and the formation of classes may be, and has been conceptualised in other ways (see Morris [1979] for a discussion of alternative approaches).

Whatever perspective is adopted, however, there are problems in attempting to relate general concepts of class and conflict to concrete historical situations; the working class is a very different kind of social group in, say, the 1880s as compared to the 1830s or the 1970s – and at any of those dates it has varying local characteristics. Historians and sociologists have increasingly recognised that it is misleading to discuss the working class – or, for that matter, any other class – as though it was a uniform, homogeneous social entity with a fixed and unchanging identity.

> 'It' – the bourgeoisie or working class – is supposed to remain the same undivided personality, albeit at different stages of maturity, throughout whole epochs; and the fact that we are discussing different people, with changing traditions, in changing relationships both as between each other and as between themselves and other social groups, becomes forgotten [Thompson, 1978, 70].

Recognition of this problem has led historians to look more closely at the internal make-up of social classes, the role of different occupational groups, and so on. If all wage-earners had some similarities of experience arising from economic insecurity and subjection to the employers' dictates, the exact forms of that experience varied, with the varying direction and timing of economic change in different industries and regions. A coherent identity was created with difficulty, through cultural and political activities that could cut across the differences.

The debate about the labour aristocracy belongs in this framework. The concept suggests that divisions within the working class were particularly marked, and took particular forms in the second half of the nineteenth century. Hobsbawm in his influential and much-quoted essay on the topic refers to 'distinctive upper strata of the working class, better paid, better treated and generally regarded as more "respectable" and politically moderate than the mass of the proletariat' [1964a, *272*]. A continuing discussion about the existence and composition of such strata is one theme in the debate about the labour aristocracy. Historians who use the concept often also suggest that the social and ideological influence of these groups was an important force in stabilising political and social relationships between classes. Different versions of this thesis vary in which groups they identify as making up the aristocracy; what they consider its defining characteristic to be; how they describe its attitudes and relations to other social groups; and how much historical weight they attach to its role. So that the discussion is more complicated than a debate between supporters and opponents of the validity of the concept of labour aristocracy; its supporters are by no means agreed among themselves, and critics of the concept would certainly not all argue that divisions within the working class did not exist or were not historically relevant.

Most uses of the concept take as their starting-point contemporary observations of trends within the working class, mostly dating from the 1850s onwards, and/or Marxist interpretations of these trends, dating from Engels (himself one of the contemporaries) and Lenin. Both Marxist analysts and contemporaries were interested in the bases of social stability in capitalist society, and the way the working class appeared to have come to terms with the basic institutions of that society. This was all the more striking in contrast to the social and political crises of the strife-torn 1830s and 40s, and the validity of such contrasts has in fact been a recurring theme of discussions about the labour aristocracy thesis. This raises broad historical questions about the development of society as a whole, the nature of stability and conflict, and the problems historians face in trying to distinguish the pattern and intensity of conflict at different periods. These issues, which arise sooner or later in any discussion about the labour aristocracy, are also at the centre of any attempt to understand the general social and political history of the decades after 1850. It will therefore be necessary to touch on a broad range of issues in any survey of the literature of the labour aristocracy debate.

Recently there has been renewed controversy about the validity of this perspective. This debate has served to clarify the varying, sometimes incompatible senses in which the term labour aristocracy is used [see especially Field, 1978 – 9; Moorhouse, 1978]. As a description of nineteenth-century urban social structure, the term is a commonplace of historical analysis, and it can also be encountered in the observations of contemporaries; as a broader explanation for patterns of British working-class development, it is more closely associated with the Marxist tradition of social analysis. Its original uses within that tradition were often polemical, arising from immediate political contexts (such as Lenin's polemic against the failure of European socialism to oppose the First World War). The uses of Marxist writers are by no means equivalent or interchangeable, although they do overlap sufficiently for many Marxist historians to work with a common body of interpretation built up from rather fragmentary comments by Marx, Engels and Lenin.

Marx's and Engels's comments can be related to a wider context of mid-Victorian observations of the declining militancy and growing fragmentation of the working class – although, as revolutionaries, they deplored what other observers welcomed [Marx and Engels, 1962 edn]. Lenin's analysis of imperialism, with which the labour aristocracy thesis is most often associated, belongs in the rather different historical context of the intensified imperialist rivalries of the 1890s and 1900s, the First World War and the collapse of the Second International. Paradoxically, however, the strongest empirical support for Lenin's view of the nature of British working-class development is drawn from the mid-Victorian years, the 'classical period' of the labour aristocracy [Hobsbawm, 1964*a*, *272*]; there are a number of problems about this backward projection of Lenin's ideas [cf. Stedman Jones, 1975, *66*]. These ideas have been interpreted subsequently with changing emphases, which reflect the political preoccupations of Marxist writers, as well as empirical historical research [Field, 1978 – 9, *67 – 8*]. The most recent reinterpretations, influenced by the ideas of the Italian Marxist thinker, Antonio Gramsci, and by the political debates of the 1960s and 70s, have criticised 'mechanistic' versions of Marxism in which it is assumed that economic forces have automatic effects in the sphere of ideas, values and political action.[1] Mechanistic Marxist approaches to the problem of the labour aristocracy would for example assume that improved economic conditions for particular sections of the working class inevitably lead to their social separation from other

11

workers and adoption of the dominant ideology of capitalist society. It should be added that such mechanistic analysis is by no means peculiar to Marxism; sociological research challenging similarly mechanistic non-Marxist arguments about the disappearance of class and the 'end of ideology' in the 1950s has in fact been another important influence in re-thinking the problem of the nineteenth-century labour aristocracy.[2] This re-thinking has led finally to questioning whether the concept of a labour aristocracy can ever be used in a way that avoids some element of mechanistic explanation, and to the suggestion that the concept should therefore be discarded altogether. This would imply a shift in emphasis to the subordinate and fragmented situation of *all* sections of the working class within a relatively stable and expanding capitalist system [see Reid, 1978].

It is thus misleading to see the debate about the labour aristocracy as a confrontation between Marxist historians and those of other persuasions. The use of the term as a description of urban social structure is widespread among historians of all persuasions; while recent criticisms of the wider explanatory uses of the term have come from writers drawing on the Marxist tradition, as well as from those who reject it. This opening of debate is in welcome contrast to the sterile polarisation that marked earlier discussions of the problem (for example Pelling [1968 chapter 3] implies that an attack on the validity of this particular hypothesis is also an attack on Marxism as such).

Some historians use the term in a purely descriptive sense, following contemporary comments on the significance of 'superior artisans' or 'the better class of working men' in industry and the community; such historians may quite legitimately sometimes be more interested in ruling-class perceptions of the working class and its effect on political debate, than in the reality corresponding to contemporary stereotypes. Others, more ambitiously but more controversially, attempt to follow Lenin's suggestions about the role of upper strata of the working class in shaping the gradualism of the British labour movement [Hobsbawm, 1964a; Foster, 1974]. There are thus two points at issue: that of the validity of attempts to identify empirically a division between labour aristocrats and other workers; and that of the wider explanatory power of such an exercise. It is the wider explanatory claims made for the concept that have been particularly under attack. Alternative explanations for working-class quiescence have been advanced, emphasising the inherent subdivision and subordination of the working class in capitalist societies [Moorhouse, 1978; Reid, 1978]. The general importance of these phenomena is not in question, but it is their working out in specific situations that is relevant for historical analysis; the historian's interest will focus on changes in the means by which a dominant class perpetuates its exploitative position and in patterns of fragmentation and cohesion in the working class, rather than on the simple fact of the rulers' domination and fragmentation among the ruled. Whatever the weaknesses of the concept of labour aristocracy, its major strength, in its application to Britain in the second half of the nineteenth century, is that it draws attention to purported features of the working class in a specific society at a specific period. (Some analysts however extend the concept to a wider geographical and chronological range, to the point where it is sometimes used as a piece of special pleading to explain away any situation in which revolutionary working-class movements fail to develop; such dubious extensions are immaterial for the purposes of the present discussion.)

It may well be true that the concept of labour aristocracy is ultimately inadequate as a model of divisions within the Victorian working class. Like any model, it can lead to the discovery of what we expect to find — especially as it is always possible to find some kind of difference between groups of workers, and to label them in this way at will — and blinker the vision so as to obscure important phenomena not reducible to the terms of the model. Sexual inequalities and the division of the labour force by age are among the important phenomena obscured by a single-minded search for 'aristocrats' and 'plebeians' of (adult male) labour. But the concept has alerted historians to the problem of subdivisions in the working class, and their consequences for relationships between classes, and generated a good deal of fruitful research.

A reassessment of the uses and limitations of the labour aristocracy is perhaps best approached through a survey of what is known — and what still remains to be discovered — about the economic positions, cultures and ideologies of different groups of workers, considered in relation to different versions of the labour aristocracy model (chapters 2 – 6 below). It is also necessary to make some rather more speculative comments on the broader explanatory uses of the model, and to consider the debate about the historical roots of working-class 'reformism' (chapters 7 and 8 below). Such a procedure will not commend itself to 'those who suppose that a successful attack upon a concept's epistemological basis is sufficient to make all those writers who have used it henceforth unreliable' [Field, 1978–9, *81*]. But if that school of thought had its way no history would ever be written. Any reformulated approach to the study of the Victorian working class will necessarily have to take account of the positive contributions of studies inspired by the labour aristocracy thesis, whatever the conclusion of further reflection about the conceptual basis of that thesis.

2 Income, Employment and Standards of Living

HISTORIANS and contemporary sources are in agreement about the existence of dramatic contrasts in the economic experience and standard of living of different working class groups. One particularly telling measure of such contrasts is their impact on the physical development of children: Rowntree's famous study of the York working class, *Poverty: a Study in Town Life* (1901), revealed that children in the more prosperous families were on average from two to three inches taller than those of the poorest group (see pp. 210–12); and information from a slightly later study by the Edinburgh Charity Organisation Society indicated similar differences within the working class [Gray, 1976, *84–5*]. The extremely low living-standards of many workers – and, as Rowntree also pointed out, many more families could expect to pass through phases of poverty over the life-cycle than fell within the poverty bracket at any given moment – made the relative, and often petty, economic advantages of the better paid and more regularly employed all the more striking. The ability to buy an evening paper might, for example, be a mark of relative comfort by working-class standards.[3] In a much-quoted passage that is nevertheless still worth citing, Rowntree conveyed vividly the significance of the subsistence standard against which he measured poverty:

> And let us clearly understand what 'merely physical efficiency' means. A family living upon the scale allowed for in this estimate must never spend a penny on railway fare or omnibus. They must never go into the country unless they walk. They must never purchase a halfpenny newspaper or spend a penny to buy a ticket for a popular concert . . . . They cannot save, nor can they join sick club or Trade Union, because they cannot pay the necessary subscriptions (pp. 133–4).

It is important to see differences in income and living-standards in

15

this perspective, and to realise that what matters is not just the absolute differential between one group and another, but also the threshold of wage-level and economic security at which workers gained wider scope for personal choice and control over their own situation [Crossick, 1978, *108*]. In reality, since no one can exist without culture, the poor *did* exercise choices, giving rise to middle-class condemnations of 'irrational' behaviour and self-induced poverty; but their choices were very narrowly circumscribed. Equally we must keep some sense of proportion in making statements about 'prosperous' occupational groups and rising standards of living. What counted as working-class prosperity was measured against the background of abject mass poverty, and those enjoying prosperity could easily disappear again into that background; by the same token, quite modest advances in consumption could appear all the more prominent [Roberts, 1971, chapter 2]. Much of the behaviour of the upper strata of the working class, especially their development of collective institutions, only makes sense in this context of proximity to a subsistence-line existence.

Discussions of the labour aristocracy have been concerned to identify groups which enjoyed this kind of relative economic advantage (though the relative aspect of the matter has not perhaps been sufficiently stressed), and to indicate the uneven impact of the general easing of pressure on real wages from about the mid-nineteenth century. The unevenness of experience is indicated by recent studies of occupational and regional depression and stagnation, associated with endemic under-employment, for instance in the sweated trades of east London clothing and Black Country metal-wares [Barnsby, 1971; Stedman Jones, 1971; Hopkins, 1975; for a perceptive contemporary analysis see Mayhew's articles reprinted in Thompson and Yeo (eds), 1971]. Nor was improvement immediate or continuous for more fortunate groups; the transition from the 'hungry forties' was a protracted and uneven process, and much of the optimistic social commentary of the 1850s and 60s was superficial and impressionistic.

Attempts to establish trends in real wages during the second half of the nineteenth century meet with problems of sources and method of similar to, but less acute than, those that complicate the continuing debate about the first half of the century. The greater stability of union organisation and the precarious institutionalisation of collective bargaining in some trades does mean that more series of standard wage-rates become available. These figures, together with those collected by official enquiries and social commentators, suggest that the greatest advances in wages were made by the skilled trades in engineering and building, various other skilled workers such as printers, some grades of railwaymen, iron and steel workers, miners, and the adult male spinners in cotton textiles. Hobsbawm, whose analysis of the labour aristocracy rests largely on such figures, notes the expansion of the capital goods sector during the second half of the century, and consequent shift in the make-up of the highest paid groups 'from the old pre-industrial crafts to the new metal industries' [1964a, 284]. The advance in skilled wages was associated with a widening of differentials, at any rate in those trades (notably engineering and building) where it is possible to compare time-rates for craftsmen with those for unskilled labourers [ibid., 292 – 5].

An approach based on wage-rates has a number of drawbacks. Most obviously, it tells us nothing about unemployment and the regularity of earnings (except in so far as severe depressions reduced standard wage-rates themselves, as certainly occurred in building and engineering). Any allowance for this will involve estimates based on a number of unknown quantities. These unknowns are particularly large for the many trades paid on piece-work systems, including hewers in mining, spinners, weavers and some other groups in textiles, most clothing and boot-and-shoe workers, compositors in printing, some shipyard trades and a growing minority of engineering workers. It should be noted that these piece-workers were generally paid entirely by output, with no guaranteed minimum; in some cases the wages of semi-skilled assistants were deducted from the piece-work 'price' of the amount produced. Where low fixed capital encouraged the employment of large numbers of semi-employed workers, piece-work earnings could fluctuate widely; in more capital-intensive sectors, the piece-workers were often among the better-paid groups.

The relationship of standard wage-rates to earnings is therefore a complicated one – still more so, in that the nature of the complications differs from one occupation to another. Analyses of wage-rates, or even of total wage-costs for a firm or industry, may moreover conceal differences within occupations which were crucial elements in defining the hierarchy of labour. Different generations might have specific experiences of improvement or decline concealed by bland generalisations about long-term trends in real wages [see Neale, 1966]. Employment records, giving information about the earnings of individual workers, can help qualify information based on wage-rates [Gray, 1976, *72–86*; Slaven, 1967]. Such studies suggest, as we might expect, that standard wage-rates may overestimate both the level and the regularity of actual earnings, and in some cases conceal differences in the position of different individuals in the same work-group. The proportion of workers at, above, or below a given wage-level is thus as important as the average wage for the occupation [Crossick, 1978, *109–10*; Cullen, 1975; Gray, 1976, *81–2*].

Studies of earnings, although they can introduce vital qualifications to trends in wage-rates, are still only a partial indicator of economic experience. This source does not indicate family circumstances or the earnings of other household members; nor does it tell us what happens to workers who disappear from the pay-roll of the firm concerned, or the reasons for their disappearance. Information that enables us to draw conclusions about the total economic condition of particular groups over substantial periods of time is scattered. Some of the growing volume of social investigation from the 1880s does, however, contain usable information about the reported incidence of unemployment, income, housing and rent, the physique of children, and so on. One survey in various parts of London in 1887 showed that occupations with above-average levels of reported unemployment included clothing, building, cabinet-making, shipwrights, unskilled labourers and dockers; with the important exceptions of the building trades and shipwrights, these were also described as low-wage occupations [Cullen, 1975]. A number of contemporary investigations, as well as recent historical studies, indicate the importance of the growth of casual labour in depressing real wages in the trade affected [Stedman Jones, 1971; Thompson and Yeo (eds), 1971; Treble, 1978]. The most notorious example was that of the docks, and of unskilled labour generally; but the problem was by no means confined to unskilled labour, also affecting tailors and shoemakers employed as sweated outworkers, especially in London where the extent of sweating was, if anything, increasing in the worst districts in the 1890s and 1900s [Schmiechen, 1975]. This was not simply an effect of seasonal variations, since some 'seasonal' trades were more successful than others in withstanding the growth of casual labour [Gray, 1976, *52 – 3, 56*].

Local diversity is a further source of difficulty in interpreting trends in living-standards. Regional wage-differentials could be as great as those between skilled and unskilled [Hunt, 1973]. The 1861 skilled engineering rate for London (35*s*.) was about fifty per cent above that for Scotland (23*s*.) [Jeffreys, 1947]. Within London itself, there were distinctive local labour markets [Hobsbawm, 1964*b*]. Most collective bargaining was local in scope, reflecting and perhaps reinforcing these regional differentials. Variations in industrial and urban structure mean that the situation of a particular occupational group has to be examined in a local context; the same industry could have wide regional variations, for example in product specialisation, markets, the level of mechanisation, and the growth of out-work and sweating. The 1887 list of depressed trades in London (quoted in the preceding paragraph) would not necessarily hold good for other times and places. Given this regional diversity, the experience of migration and the adaptability of an individual's skills to more advanced and specialised sectors of industrial expansion were cruicial to the economic experience of skilled labour. Differences within occupations could be as important as those between occupations.

Any attempt to identify potential labour aristocrats among high-paid workers must take account of these complexities. Despite all the difficulties, it is possible to point to groups (such as skilled engineers) who made marked advances in the second half of the nineteenth century, and to others (such as the sweated clothing and shoe trades) who suffered stagnation or actual decline. This is not in itself surprising, or peculiar to the period; the whole history of industrial capitalism suggests that 'labour was not a homogeneous lump but a variegated amalgam' [Burgess, 1975, *307*]. A recurrent problem with analyses of the labour aristocracy is that it is possible at any period to find *some* workers whose real incomes are increasing faster than others. To establish what is specific to the mid- and late-Victorian period, it is necessary to look more closely at the organisation of production in different industries, and the roles of different occupations in the labour process.

3 Skills and the Division of Labour

NINETEENTH-CENTURY industry was very diverse in its levels of mechanisation, scale of operation, subdivision of processes, and so on. In a classic passage of his *Economic History of England* (1932, vol. *II*. chapter 2). Clapham pointed to the prevalence of small units and unmechanised methods about 1850, and this diversity persisted throughout the century [see Samuel, 1977]. This has long been noted by historians, but its significance is less fully examined; unmechanised sectors are often seen as purely 'traditional', as yet unaffected by the processes of industrial change. But it is becoming clear from recent research – as it was to some contemporaries, such as Henry Mayhew and Karl Marx – that non-mechanised labour could undergo radical changes in its organisation and its location within the wider system of economic relations [Stedman Jones, 1971; Marx, 1976 edn, chapter 15; Thompson and Yeo (eds), 1971].

This modern 'domestic industry' has nothing except the name in common with old-fashioned domestic industry, the existence of which presupposes independent urban handicrafts, independent peasant farming and, above all, a dwelling-house for the worker and his family. That kind of industry has now been converted into an external department of the factory, the manufacturing workshop, or the warehouse [Marx, 1976, *591*].

Equally features of the 'craft' division of labour might be reproduced within a large-scale mechanised production process [Robertson, 1974, 1975; Melling, 1980]. There were moreover complex relationships between mechanised and unmechanised sectors; in the Birmingham metal trades, for example, the hiring out of steam-power in small workshops was associated with increased time-discipline and a consequent transformation of leisure [Reid, 1976]. The economic position of occupational groups was conditioned by their ability to define bargaining-positions within an industrial division of labour that was changing in a variety of complicated ways; this process of definition involved conflicts over autonomy and control in the work-place, as well as over wages and hours [Field, 1978–9, 79].

Economic differences within the working class have therefore to be placed in the context of the social and technical organisation of work. Historians have begun to pay closer attention to the way the 'labour process' was structured, and to explore systematically industrial variations and the precise chronology and incidence of change. This is not just a matter of technology and the gradual spread of more 'advanced' techniques. The adoption of particular methods, the utilisation of machines and workers, the size of units of production, types of product and amount produced, forms of wage-payment and so on, did not just depend on what might be technically possible. A number of social and economic conditions were also relevant: notably the market position of the industry and the particular firm, the balance of power between employers and workers, and relations between groups of workers [*Cambridge Journal of Economics*, 1979; Hobsbawm, 1964a, chapter 17]. The heavy dependence of key sectors of nineteenth-century industry on skilled labour was a function of all these things.

Engineering, building, various urban crafts, mining and cotton-spinning have all figured prominently in accounts of the labour aristocracy, and the following discussion will look briefly and schematically at each of these industries, before mentioning some general problems in attempting to draw comparative conclusions about the structure of the Victorian working class.

(i) ENGINEERING

The engineering industry is often regarded as central to the formation of a labour aristocracy. The expansion of the industry, and of the capital goods sector generally, was certainly associated with an expansion of skilled employment, much of it highly paid especially in boom years. The position of skilled engineering workers had been under pressure in the 1840s and early 50s, culminating in the lock-out of 1852 [Jeffreys, 1945, 35–9; Burgess, 1969]. Thereafter, however, the pace of technical change slackened (at least until the 1890s), a high rate of investment taking the form of diversification and the spread of the new techniques from their narrow base in Lancashire and the West Riding. A booming overseas market for machinery, protected by Britain's lead in techniques and productive capacity, eased the pressure on employers; the character of these markets encouraged skilled labour-intensive 'one-off' production, rather than mass production for stock [Burgess, 1975, *25 – 6*]. Despite the defeat of the ASE (Amalgamated Society of Engineers) in the 1852 lock-out, the success of 'advanced' firms in Lancashire in breaking trade custom and imposing piece-work and systematic overtime was not repeated elsewhere; and even where these practices did prevail they were subject to regulation, with piece-work earnings floating above the 'floor' of the standard time-rate [Jeffreys, 1947].

In these circumstances the industry was heavily dependent on the skilled labour of fitters and turners; the continuing importance of craft skill, for example, inhibited the development of formal technical education [Robertson, 1974]. Management's authority was limited by craft custom; foremen retained their trade affiliations (often belonging to the same craft unions), and were only slowly and painfully transformed into a distinct supervisory stratum [Melling, 1980]. This situation was not automatically assured, nor did the much-quoted industrial pacifism of the ASE imply an absence of conflict in the workshops [Murphy, 1978; see chapter 6 below for a discussion of craft union strategies in the period]. There was constant friction about the piecemeal introduction of new methods, and the manning of machines, as well as attempts to increase wages and shorten the working day; conflicts intensified as the equilibrium of the mid-Victorian period was shaken towards the end of the century, with new competitive pressures and further technical changes [Jeffreys, 1945, *122 – 44*]. However these developments, like those of the 1840s and early 50s, were more marked in some regions than others, and the entrenched position of apprentice-trained craftsmen remained intact in many engineering centres. Just as in 1852, a serious defeat for the ASE in the lock-out of 1897 – 8 did not lead to the destruction of the union's power, nor to that of the skilled trades it represented.

(ii) BUILDING

Building is often cited as a classic case of a 'traditional' sector growing to provide the infrastructure of an urban-industrial society [Burgess, 1975, chapter 2; Crossick, 1978, *73*; Gray, 1976, *37*]. But, as in other sectors of Victorian industry, a focus on the absence of large-scale mechanisation can obscure important changes in the organisation of work and a consequent growth of specialisation and occupational subdivision. Although the common impression of very small-scale employment – and of a relatively 'open' route from journeyman to small master – may be accurate, these immediate units were implicated in a web of subcontract, while the partial standardisation of methods and materials diminished the versatility of many craftsmen. By the 1900s wood-working and stone-cutting machines, new materials such as concrete and steel, and acute depression in the industry were undermining craft controls. The piecemeal application of machines was typical of the changes occurring in labour-intensive crafts in the second half of the nineteenth century, with effects on the pace of work, the versatility and initiative of skilled labour and the possibility of 'dilution'.

The position of building craftsmen depended on their ability to maintain trade boundaries in the face of these pressures. Heavy seasonal unemployment, and cyclical swings in building activity added to the threat of casual labour and erosion of craft practices. There is considerable diversity among the various trades, and also 'professional gradations' [Gray, 1976, *37*] within each trade. Painters, the 'ragged-trousered philanthropists' of Robert Tressell's novel of that title (written in the 1900s; first published in full in 1955), were notoriously a low-paid, casualised and diluted trade; joiners, bricklayers and masons, despite vulnerability to seasonal unemployment, often appear in the better-paid and more secure section of the working class [Crossick, 1978, *74, 109 – 11*; Gray, 1976, *63 – 7*].

(iii) URBAN CRAFTS

A number of skilled trades were characterised, like building, by their relationship to an expanding urban market, the most skilled employment often being for a luxury or bespoke end of that market. Here again, the absence of large-scale mechanisation should not be taken to imply an absence of any change in methods of production. In printing the steam-powered press was a skill-intensive method (which if anything raised the level of skill, as compared to the old hand press), and hand-labour continued to prevail in the typesetting process, in the context of concentration into larger units and intensified division of labour. In Edinburgh, a major centre for publishing and printing, divisions emerged between a minority of compositors paid on time-rates, and a larger group of less regularly employed men paid on piece-rates [Gray, 1976, *57 – 62*]. In the clothing and shoemaking trades, the process of casualisation was more marked, with a substantial sector of sweated labour, working at home with no customary or trade union controls of wages and conditions. Other urban crafts were more successful in retaining some control over the re-structuring of the labour process, adapting to and partly shaping changes in the division of labour. Such trades included most printers, book binders, the better end of the clothing and furniture trades, coachmakers, jewellers, watchmakers, and so on; although each of these might be quite small in any town, together they accounted for a substantial sector of employment, with a visible social presence in the urban community and the institutions of organised labour. They were especially important in the national capitals of Edinburgh and London, and probably in regional commercial and administrative centres, from small market towns to the commercial metropolises of the industrial north and midlands.

Workers in such trades were often employed in very small units, with rather limited application of machines or steam-power. This does not mean, however, that they enjoyed a 'traditional' situation, unaffected by industrial change; their security rested on their ability to control changes in the division of labour. In many urban crafts the labour force consisted mostly of time-served skilled men, together with apprentices. They had considerable autonomy and control in the workshop, and could protect their position by strong trade customs [see Gilding, 1971].

(iv) MINING

In the trades so far discussed craft skills transmitted by formal apprenticeship were essential to the production process; while apprenticeship may have been eroded by subdivision, casualisation and mechanisation, craft training – including the ability to adapt to new methods – remained important for the better-paid and more regularly employed section in each trade. The analysis of skill and division of labour becomes more complicated in those industries, such as mining and textiles,

24

without formal systems of apprenticeship.

Coal-mining expanded rapidly during the second half of the nineteenth century with the increasing use of steam-power, urban demand for house-coal, and the beginings from the 1870s of a thriving export market. Although the industry involved large capital outlays, these were in the sinking of shafts, winding-gear and transport facilities from the pit-head; the actual cutting of coal depended on arduous hand-labour with a pick, and the physical isolation of workers at the coal-face gave them a high degree of independence from supervisory control [Burgess, 1975, *154 – 5*]. Where the hewers (the men who actually cut the coal) had the necessary cohesion and organisation to develop a 'quasi-craft' position in the work-place this strengthened their bargaining-power; elsewhere employers were able to prevent this development by fostering competition for employment and individual undercutting of piece-work rates (which had complicated variations to allow for geological conditions, the difficulty of working, and so on). The various coalfields, but also villages and pits in the same region, differed widely in this respect; but everywhere the hewers' position was made less secure by recruitment of additional labour from agriculture and immigration, market fluctuations, and undercutting competition between firms and coalfields [Harrison (ed.), 1978].

The diversity of the industry makes generalisation difficult. Coalfields varied in their product (steam- or house-coal, or both), markets, size and depth of working, concentration of ownership, methods of working and payment, and so on [Burgess, 1975, chapter 3; Harrison (ed.), 1978]. The precise pattern of subdivision in the labour force, relations between grades of worker and recruitment to the best-paid jobs (always the hewers) varied, and in many cases remain obscure. The principal division was that between the hewers, other underground workers engaged in haulage etc., and pit-head workers. The hewers were adult men, while the other grades included many boys (whose chances of becoming hewers, and subordination to the hewers' authority pose important questions in the analysis of mine labour)[4] and, at the pit-head, women and girls. The hierarchy of mine labour was thus partly one of age and sex – the strength and endurance of work at the coal-face perhaps became identified with the cult of masculinity.

Where the hewers could take advantage of their control of the immediate work situation they were in a relatively strong bargaining-position. Again, there were wide regional differences. The Durham and Northumberland coalfields, partly because of their early development and long established traditions of organisation and struggle, had strong organisations dominated by the hewers [Burgess, 1975, *180 – 2*]; in Scotland, attempts to build organisation based on traditions of independence and craft control repeatedly failed [A. Campbell, 'Honourable Men and Degraded Serfs', in Harrison (ed.), 1978]; the Black Country miners shared the generally depressed wage-levels of that region [Barnsby, 1971; Hopkins, 1975]. The real wages of hewers in the strongest regions and pits or in the best years perhaps approximated to those of skilled labour – as in many respects did the values and attitudes associated with their organisations [Harrison (ed.), 1978; Slaven, 1967].

(v) COTTON

Cotton textiles was of course the first sector of industry to develop mechanised mass production, and it remained the most important 'factory' industry throughout the nineteenth century. It was strongly localised to the north-west of England, and the 'cotton towns' were seen as distinctive industrial communities, differing from other urban-industrial areas and from each other; there was broad specialisation into spinning and weaving districts, and within this a concentration of coarser or finer types of work [Burgess, 1975, *235 – 6*]. The factory labour force was heterogeneous, with sex and age often regulating the division of labour. The best-paid workers were the adult male spinners, about a fifth of the total spinning labour force, who minded the machines and supervised the work of the semi-skilled piecers (mainly boys and men); spinners were recruited from the piecers, and it was the regulation of this process that maintained the spinners' position [Burgess, 1975, *236 – 40*; Liddington and Norris, 1978, chapter 5]. Women were employed in preparatory processes in the carding and blowing room. In weaving, which was sometimes integrated in the same plant as spinning but more often separate and localised to the northern part of the cotton area, more women were employed alongside some men; the better-paid types of loom were generally allocated to men, creating a sex differential in wages despite a single piece-work list [Liddington and Norris, 1978, *92 – 9*].

Earnings were regulated by complicated piece-lists, with workplace conflict centering on the speed of machines, the number of spindles or looms per operative, and allowances for lower-grade raw material.

The structure of the labour force did not simply reflect the technical requirements of mechanised production. It was also shaped by problems of supervision and control, the strategies of employers under given market conditions, the sexual division of labour, and the bargaining-power of groups of workers. Supervisory functions and the need for certain specialised skills were the basis for the position of the mule-spinners, despite the apparent erosion of their skills by technical change; the system of payment, whereby spinners' piece-work earnings varied with output while the piecers' time-rate wages did not, made for a measure of co-operation in raising productivity and intensifying labour [W. Lazonick, 'Industrial Relations and Technical Change', in *Cambridge Journal of Economics*, 1979]. With the greater economic stability of the mid-Victorian period the spinners, on the basis of this strategic role in production, were able to advance their economic position and establish tight controls over manning and recruitment of labour, excluding women and carefully regulating boys and men. 'Skill' was thus a function of the balance of industrial power and cultural attitudes, although it would be wrong to conclude that it was entirely an artificial creation [Stedman Jones, 1975, *52 – 3*; Turner, 1962; cf. Lazonick in *Cambridge Journal of Economics*, 1979].

The availability of well-paid jobs (by the standards of female and juvenile wages elsewhere) for women and children meant, on the other hand, that family real incomes were higher for all sectors of the labour force than in other regions [Anderson, 1971, chapters 10, 11; Foster, 1974, *91 – 9*]. The relationship between employment and family structure is thus of crucial importance, complicating any attempt to draw analogies with 'skilled' and 'unskilled' labour elsewhere [Joyce, 1975].

(vi) CONCLUSIONS

There is considerable diversity in the structure of Victorian industry. This poses difficulties for any attempt to define a common hierarchy of labour, and to identify a potential labour aristocracy in its upper levels. The definition of skilled and unskilled labour is a good deal less straightforward than it might seem. This becomes clear in looking at mining and cotton, but it is also true in other industries; many problems can be concealed by apparently unambiguous distinctions between craftsmen and labourers. The definition of tasks as skilled work – and always by implication adult men's work – was not simply a matter of their technical content, but also of conflict over the boundaries of skill. Groups with traditions of craft organisation could make the availability of special skills conditional on an employment monopoly over a range of intrinsically less skilled operations – to the constant exasperation of, for example, engineering employers. Conversely in almost every 'unskilled' job there was some element of on-the-job training which enhanced the value of experienced workers. Such experience was especially important in mining where the danger of inexperienced men underground was a frequent argument against the introduction of additional labour. Another important element, in an age when employers and the ruling class generally were concerned about the moral condition of the poor, was that of responsibility and trust in such jobs as the railways, postal services, and so on. The reward for loyalty, trustworthiness and submission to a draconian corporate discipline (symbolised in the wearing of uniforms) was a regularity of employment exceptional for unskilled labour [Kingsford, 1970]. This element of perceived reliability and trust could also be important in skilled trades, especially for those groups often referred to as 'superior artisans'.

Further problems are posed by the role of sex discrimination in the labour market, and its complicated relationship to the division of labour between the sexes in the home and society as a whole. The exclusion of women was one means of policing the frontiers of craft skill. There was a consequent tendency to regard any work performed by women as by definition unskilled – and therefore requiring less payment – regardless of the content of the particular job [Alexander, 1976; Taylor, 1977]. Outside textile mills, women's employment was concentrated in domestic service (which they normally had to leave on marriage), and a range of sweated trades which took advantage of the captive labour market of women confined to the home. Such women provided 'a "reserve army of labour", a casual labour force which could be utilised to supply the exigencies of economic fluctuations' [Taylor, 1977,

28

51–2]. Often, as in the Nottingham lace trade [ibid., *49*], the casual out-work of women was combined with a more stable factory sector in which men monopolised the best jobs.

This employment pattern reproduced and reinforced a sexual division of labour in the family and society as a whole; women's employment was seen as marginal and not requiring to earn a 'breadwinner's' income. The relationship of employment to sexual divisions is thus an important dimension of differentiation within the working class – and one that concentration on occupational divisions between potential 'aristocrats' and others has tended to obscure. The pattern of variations within the working class in family structures and roles and the reasons for it remain largely obscure [but see Anderson, 1971]. But it would certainly seem that the subordinate role of women at all social levels was an important factor in shaping, and sometimes cutting across the occupational hierarchy of manual labour.

4 Who Were the 'Labour Aristocrats'?

EVERY trade and industry contained superior groupings of workers, enjoying higher pay, greater economic security, and often a large measure of control in the immediate work situation. It is in such features that historians have identified the basis for a labour aristocracy. This analysis has perhaps been most successful at the level of specific occupations and localities; the diversity of industrial and urban social structure presents problems in generalising, or trying to draw analogies between groups of workers in different situations. Hence definitions of the make-up of the aristocratic upper stratum have varied, and 'the use of this idea has been ambiguous and unsatisfactory . . . . Indicative of its lack of precision is the elasticity of the stratum of the working class referred to' [Stedman Jones, 1975, *61*].

Hobsbawm, in a much-cited passage, mentions a number of criteria by which to distinguish members of the labour aristocracy:

> *First,* the level and regularity of a worker's earnings; *second,* his prospects of social security; *third,* his conditions of work, including the way he was treated by foremen and masters; *fourth,* his relations with the social strata above and below him; *firth,* his general conditions of living; *lastly,* his prospects of future advancement and those of his children [Hobsbawn, 1964*a*, *273*].

This essay (originally published in 1954) marked an important advance in the empirical application of the concept to historical research, and has been the starting-point for many subsequent studies. This approach has been a fruitful one, but it also has certain limitations. The difficulty with listing criteria in this way is that it is always possible to discover *some* social and economic differentiation in the working class along the dimensions specified.

This does not in itself provide any guide to defining distinct social groups: how great do differences have to be, and what form do they have to take, to enable us to talk of a labour aristocracy?

Hobsbawm does also suggest one line of approach to defining the historically distinctive feature of the labour aristocracy. He refers to the persistence of craft methods in many sectors of British industry, the potential bargaining-power this afforded to key groups of workers, and the significance of 'artisan' cultures and modes of activity in the formation of the working class [this is suggested in the essay on the labour aristocracy, but more explicitly developed in other essays: ibid., *278 – 84, 290 – 5*, see also especially chapters 4, 16, 17]. This echoes Engels's comments, in which he points to the textile operatives (protected by factory legislation) and 'those trades in which the labour of *grown-up men* predominates' as relatively advantaged groups; like Hobsbawm, Engels identifies the upper stratum largely with the membership of the 'great Trades' Unions' [Marx and Engels, 1962 edn, 28; cf. Hobsbawm, 1964*a*, *280*].

The recent debate about the labour aristocracy has centred on issues of work organisation, and especially on the continuities and discontinuities of industrial development in the early- to mid-nineteenth century. Thus Foster [1974] argues that the basis for the emergence of a new upper stratum lies in changes in industrial structure and especially in the system of authority in the workplace. His labour aristocrats are piece-workers in engineering, spinners in cotton and checkweighmen in mining; all these, he suggests, represented new forms of industrial authority emerging in the 1850s and acting very much as the agents of capital in supervising, 'pace-setting' and disciplining the rest of the workforce. This analysis has been widely discussed. Attention has been drawn to the limited extent of piece-work in engineering outside Oldham (where the great lock-out of 1852 in fact had its origins in disputes at the exceptionally 'advanced' firm of Hibbert & Platt), the relationship of occupation to family structure in cotton, and the trade union base of checkweighmen in the better organised coalfields [Field, 1978 – 9, *78*].

In a stimulating and influential review of Foster, Stedman Jones [1975] argues that the transition to a more stable industrial capitalism with an expanding sector of mechanised production involved the adaptation of *all* parts of the labour force to effective capitalist control of production. The traditional autonomy of craftsmen was destroyed, but divisions of skill were then re-created and maintained by groups with the necessary bargaining-power. Other contributions have suggested that both Foster and Stedman Jones may be working with an over-general, once-for-all view of the transition to industrial capitalism. The impact of capitalist development, especially in the nineteenth century, was not simply to destroy skills, but to create the basis for new forms of skilled labour, within which craft methods and traditions could assert themselves [see *Cambridge Journal of Economics*, 1979; Melling, 1980]. Attempts to rationalise production were limited by the strength of skilled labour, market conditions, and the absence of managerial experience; the prospectuses of inventors and entrepreneurs might promise to eliminate independent and wilful skilled men, what actually happened as machinery was introduced was another matter. To accept areas of craft control over production could also appear a more viable strategy than grandiose schemes of rationalisation, especially with the limited character of managerial technique. Thus the position of machine-minders in cotton-spinning rested partly on the indispensability of their supervisory role and the costs of eliminating certain core skills [Lazonick in *Cambridge Journal of Economics*, 1979]. Although skill is partly a question of bargaining-power and cultural attitudes, there were few if any groups of skilled workers whose position did not involve control of some specialised technique indispensable to their employers – that control was indeed the basis of their bargaining-power.

A further set of issues is concerned with historical continuities and discontinuities, the extent to which this role of skilled labour was, as the labour aristocracy thesis generally implies, leading to the formation of new groupings within the working class, rather than simply to the perpetuation of earlier artisan traditions. The earliest uses of the term 'aristocracy of labour' in fact refer to hierarchies within certain crafts, such as coachmaking, in the 1830s and 40s. The labour aristocracy described by historians of the third quarter of the century may therefore simply represent the expansion and flourishing of these same groups under the favourable conditions of a long up-swing in the trade cycle. There can be no doubt of the cultural importance of traditions drawn from the artisan cultures of the 1830s and before, or of the economic importance of the apprenticed skills drawn from these older trades. But there were also newer trades, especially those associated with engineering, shipbuilding and the rapid expansion of capital goods production generally, which altered the occupational make-up of the working class. It would, moreover, be wrong to suppose that the persistence of craft methods in the older trades indicated an absence of change and adaptation to change. Those trades which managed to stabilise their position did so by exerting some control over processes of mechanisation (often piecemeal mechanisation in small workshops) and/or new forms of intensified division of labour; those which failed succumbed to technological unemployment or the casualisation of employment. Too little attention has been paid to these processes, outside the key exporting industries of textiles and capital goods, and it is difficult to draw firm conclusions about the nature of change and responses to it. As with any historical problem, continuity versus discontinuity is a far too clear-cut and polarised question; it is a matter of disentangling in detail aspects of continuity and change.

One consequence of a closer examination of the labour process in different industries may be to introduce heavy qualifications of any attempt to generalise about the structure of the working class. Groups with similar levels of pay, and all thinking of themselves as 'artisans', might have different roles in the production process, different relations to less skilled groups, and so on [Reid, 1978]. Sexual divisions between male and female labour, or practices of ethnic or religious exclusion [Lunn (ed.), 1980] cannot be treated in the same terms as purely occupational divisions between craftsmen and (adult male) labourers; although in some cases these different forms of division might be mutually reinforcing, in others they cut across each other. Any attempt to identify a potential labour aristocracy must take account of these complexities.

One way out of these difficulties may be to look at the formation of social groups in local contexts. Working-class experience and behaviour are not confined to the work-place, and the basis for a cohesive upper stratum within the working class has also to be sought in the local community; the same occupational groups may act differently in different community settings. This implies a shift in emphasis from economic and industrial structures to culture and community, values and life-styles [see for example Crossick, 1978; Gray, 1976]. Such studies have tried to show the formation of a labour aristocracy, or 'artisan élite', through local institutions which drew together men from a range of trades, but still tended to set them apart from less advantaged sections of the working class. Other types of organisation, including friendly societies, co-ops, sports clubs, churches, and so on, have been used to add a further dimension to the emphasis on trade union organisation as a characteristic of the labour aristocracy. There is certainly strong evidence for the heavy representation of certain skilled trades in this range of local movements, and for the projection of a sense of social identity through that involvement; and it seems to be those trades, such as skilled engineers and some building crafts, in relatively strong economic positions which are especially prominent in this process. But, like other attempts to identify labour aristocrats, this meets with problems of generalisation. Such patterns may be peculiar to certain types of town: London, Edinburgh, and perhaps various regional capitals, marked by an infrastructure of service and consumer trades, especially those with a large 'luxury' market [see Field, 1978 – 9, 76].

There are thus difficulties and limitations in all the competing definitions of the aristocratic stratum. Whilst there are certainly wide differences within the working class, it is difficult to relate them in any systematic way to the social relations of work in industry, or to formulate models that can take account of industrial and regional variations. Nor are the patterns of differentiation necessarily peculiar, as some treatments of the labour aristocracy would suggest, to the second half of the nineteenth century. On the other hand, there is considerable evidence of processes of subdivision within the working class, and it may be that these were peculiarly intense under the conditions of the mid-Victorian boom and the uneven incidence of mechanisation in British industry. It is perhaps more important to examine these tendencies, to which the labour aristocracy thesis has rightly drawn attention, than to attempt to arrive at cut-and-dried definitions of the membership of social strata. The pursuit of precise definition can run the risk of imposing a static model on what is in reality a dynamic historical process.

5 Culture and Ideology

IN analysing industrial structure and economic differences it is essential to avoid taking for granted the cultural processes which, according to all versions of the labour aristocracy thesis, were linked to economic differences (Hobsbawm, 1964a, seems open to this criticism). Broader reappraisals of 'class' as a historical category, which emphasise cultural and political elements in class consciousness, have contributed to a re-thinking of the problem of the labour aristocracy. The economic developments of the mid-Victorian period are seen as 'a *necessary* but not a *sufficient* condition for the formation of the labour aristocracy'; hence 'we have to look . . . for evidence that this elite of skilled men actually took on exclusive values, patterns of behaviour and social aspirations that effectively distinguished it from other sections of society' [Crossick, 1978, *18 – 19*]. One aspect of this problem has been the recognition of urban social structure and local community as an important dimension, shaping the context for the development of working-class values and aspirations.

This is often approached, explicitly or implicitly, in terms of concepts of 'social status' derived ultimately from Max Weber. For Weber, 'society was stratified into a series of status groups distinguished by common life styles and social evaluation' [Morris, 1979, *62*]; such things as residential patterns and inter-marriage marked the boundaries of groups which subdivided or cut across the major economically defined social classes.[5] Studies of housing, marriage, and participation in voluntary associations such as sports clubs or churches do indicate a separation of skilled workers from the unskilled on the one hand, and some contact with white-collar and small business groups of the local lower-middle class on the other [Crossick, 1978 chapters 6 – 9; Foster, 1974, *126 – 9, 211*; Gray, 1976, chapters 5, 6]. Perhaps more significantly, there is some evidence that this pattern varies between skilled occupations themselves, being most marked in those trades presented, on economic grounds, as candidates for membership of the labour aristocracy [see for example Gray, 1976, 107]. But the pattern is by no means clear-cut. Skilled workers suffering casualisation might, like the Northampton shoemakers, maintain their separate identity and commitment to 'respectability' [Foster, 1974, 129 – 30; and cf Gray, 1976, 113 – 15]. There is also, as with all local-based studies, the problem of generalisation. The separation off of artisan élites may be characteristic of certain types of locality, while other types had different patterns. Thus Joyce [1975] has argued that the cotton towns were unified culturally by the effects of family employment and the acceptance of the employers' social leadership. Ethnic and/or religious divisions could add a further locally variable dimension to sub-grouping within the working class [Campbell in Harrison (ed.), 1978; Foster, 1974, 128 – 9; Lunn, (ed.), 1980].

The wider interpretation of indices of social distance remains ambiguous. As with wage differentials, it is invariably possible to detect *some* degree of differentiation between groups of workers; but *how much* difference constitutes a separate labour aristocracy or artisan élite? One problem with 'neo-Weberian' approaches is the implied assumption that status, which for Weber had connotations of 'social honour' and deference by status inferiors, has the same significance in widely divergent social situations and is measurable by observed statistical patterns of social contact.[6] But the wider significance of these phenomena varies; the fact that, for example, people marry partners of rather similar social background may or may not imply conscious exclusion of, or contempt for, other groups. Any statistical approach runs the risk of 'mindless quantification' unless it is related to evidence about values, aspirations and social meanings. The commonly cited indices of social distance have therefore to be interpreted with caution. At all periods of its history the working class is marked by tendencies to fragmentation, as well as by some unity of social experience and activity; it is changes in the relative importance of these tendencies that matter. Thus Foster [1974, chapter 7] uses indices of social distance to argue for a growing fragmentation of the Oldham working class from the 1850s, and relates this to a broader context of changes in industrial structure and political activity.

Measures of social distance are significant, in so far as they form part of a wider pattern. We have to look at the ways in which groups constructed social identities for themselves, and the extent to which those identities were expressed in social life and institutions and met with some recognition in the wider community. This cultural process is not susceptible to precise measurement, but has to be reconstructed from a more 'qualitative' analysis of language and social imagery. It is often suggested that the notion of a labour aristocracy, far from being an invention of Marxist historians, is widespread in contemporary sources [for example Harrison, 1965, 5]. It is certainly possible to encounter the term. But such expressions as 'respectable artisans' or 'the better class of working men' were more common [for examples, see Gray, 1976, 96, 121 – 2]. Interpretation of this social imagery encounters the familiar problem of the predominance in most sources of observation of working-class life and attitudes from above. However it is worth noting that such distinctions are also articulated from within the working class, or at any rate from observers still close to the experience of manual labour. Thomas Wright, the 'journeyman engineer', was concerned to refute ignorance of the complex social distinctions of the world of skilled labour: 'There is no typical working man . . . . People who talk of the working man would, if questioned upon the point, be found to have in their mind's-eye either an ideal conception or some particular type of working man' [Wright, 1970, 5 – 6]. Statements of this kind do suggest widespread recognition of social differences within the working class, although one must beware of assuming that contemporary expressions are interchangeable, either with each other or with more recent analytical uses of the term labour aristocracy.

'Respectability' was an important theme in contemporary social images. Social historians have come to recognise the centrality of respectability as a value held, in different forms, by a wide range of groups in Victorian society [see especially Best, 1971]. It was closely bound up with 'independence', the ability to provide for oneself and one's family in whatever style was appropriate to a particular social level and to avoid the indignities of subjection to 'the will and dictates of others' [Crossick, 1978, 136]. For the middle class, this could mean ownership and control of one's means of livelihood, however modest, or possibly the status of monthly as opposed to weekly wage-payment; for the working class, independence 'need not conflict with wage-employment, for many of the subtleties of status rested upon degrees of craft control in the workplace' [ibid]. Such ideas have sometimes been interpreted in terms of the downward transmission of bourgeois ideology, and it is certainly true that a version of respectability was central to bourgeois attitudes and values. But, like all words in wide circulation, respectability had different meanings for different groups of people, as they adapted it to their own situation. Values of respectability may indeed originate partly within the working class – or its 'pre-industrial' predecessors. In its popular meanings, the term could imply self-respect, and self-control as the precondition of a struggle to exert control over the conditions of one's life, expressed in collective rather than purely individual forms. Working-class respectability was more ambiguous than a passive reception of middle-class indoctrination; in so far as it meant self-respect and the independence of working-class institutions at a collective level, it was a two-edged sword.

Rising standards of housing and domestic comfort contributed to the image of the 'respectable artisan'. The conditions of the home and deficiencies of working-class family life were a major focus of social concern in ruling-class opinion, and the apparent conformity of some sections of the working class to ideals of domesticity was one source of mid-Victorian social optimism; a spokesman for the building society movement in Birmingham claimed at the Royal Commission on Friendly Societies: 'They go home at night and cultivate their gardens, or read the newspapers to their wives, instead of being in public-houses. We are the greatest social reformers of the day' [Parliamentary Papers, 1871, XXV, q. 3746]. Such values no doubt belong to the interpretation from above of working-class behaviour and aspirations – the desire to live in a better house does not in itself imply these deeper meanings, and home-ownership could represent an escape from the insecurity and dependence of rented housing [cf. Crossick, 1978, *148–9*]. But ideologies of independence and domestic respectability were certainly present within the working class, bound up with the escape from conditions of degradation and dependence within the housing market, through 'the reinforcing nature of economic capability and personal values, for the desire for home ownership was itself seen as a criterion for being a respectable and superior working man' [ibid.].

This had important implications for the role of women, defined in primarily domestic terms, and the corresponding definition of the male wage as the family 'breadwinner'. Thomas Wright [1970] devoted a chapter to 'workingmen's wives and homes', bemoaning the low level of household skill and its effects on domestic comfort. Differences in family roles within the working class, and their connections with employment conditions and value systems need further study [but see Anderson, 1971; Davidoff, 1974; Taylor, 1977]. One problem is the familiar one of the relationship of working-class behaviour to middle-class efforts at moral and social improvement, which were in many cases centrally concerned with the stability of family life conceived in terms of dominant values. Such values were often expressed in a language common to bourgeois reformers and philanthropists and would-be 'respectable' workers. But, as with other aspects of working-class respectability, it is important to recognise that particular forms of behaviour were also, and perhaps primarily, responses to a given economic and social environment – including the structuring of local institutions in terms of the values of middle-class groups, with consequent pressures on working people to demonstrate their conformity. Economic structure and ideology were mutually reinforcing, in perpetuating the sexual division of labour in industry, the home and society. The exclusion of women, and the demand for a breadwinner's wage for men was an industrial bargaining strategy, enabling men to make sectional gains while women provided employers with a pool of casual labour at below-subsistence wages. For women confronted by the limited opportunities of this labour market, marriage could offer better chances of survival [Taylor, 1977]; moreover the time devoted to household tasks could have an appreciable effect on the living-standards of even the poorest families [Roberts, 1977]. Hence ideologies of domesticity did not simply function as abstract ideas, but were embedded in the material conditions of working-class life.

The study of life-styles and leisure activities has been one fruitful approach to distinctions between working-class strata. Changes in the organisation of leisure during the nineteenth century have been seen in relation to attempts to impose social discipline and adaptation to the conditions of industrial production. It is however easier to discuss the intentions of dominant groups than the responses of working people [see Donajgrodzki (ed.), 1977; Reid, 1976]. Urban life-styles, and the strategies adopted by those seeking to exert power and influence, were themselves shaped by the active responses of working people, and it is necessary to beware of some of the static and manipulative implications of concepts of 'social control' [Stedman Jones, 1977]. The commitment of upper strata of the working class to respectability reflects this active response, rather than passive reception of bourgeois propaganda [Crossick, 1978, *151 – 6*; Gray, 1976, chapter 7; and cf. Morris, 1979, *60 – 1*]. In so far as values were shared, class tension could be expressed in diverging interpretations of a common language. One example of this is the way that those groups most capable economically of adopting behaviour fostered by middle-class 'reformers' – saving, self-education, improved housing, and so on – were also most insistent on their own identity, most resistant to the heavy-handed patronage of many efforts at voluntary social improvement. In the working men's clubs, for example, there was a sharp conflict over demands to achieve organisational independence of the clergy and other philanthropic patrons [Price, 1971].

Different strata of the working class are perhaps distinguished less by adherence to these values, than by the capacity to express them in institutional form. Friendly societies, the co-operative movement, working men's clubs, and so on, established a recognised presence in the urban community, and contributed to the image of working-class prosperity and self-improvement; trade unionism also won a more grudging and halting acceptance, but the problems surrounding this demand separate discussion (below, chapter 6). Such institutions were not in themselves new. But, with changes in the wider economic, social and political context, they gained greater stability and legitimacy in ruling-class opinion; at the same time they became less 'open', more closely identified with limited aspirations and more or less narrow strata within the working class. The wider aspirations of co-operation became less prominent, with increased concentration on business-like retailing and financial stability [Pollard, 1960]. Quite apart from any feelings about social status, the demands of economic viability made for a limited clientele [Yeo, 1976, *286*]. This does not mean that the earlier traditions were wiped out; but they continued in a different context, with new constraints and new opportunities. Although some form of saving was far more widespread than bourgeois moralists would allow, savings institutions were themselves differentiated, and those with the greatest stability, security and benefit seem to have had a narrower social base [Crossick, 1978, chapter 9; Levitt and Smout, 1979, *129–31*].

Recent research has called into question stereotypes of a deferential and indoctrinated labour aristocracy. While self-assertion certainly occurred within a broader acceptance of the social framework, and an expectation that working-class claims could be accommodated in that framework, it also reflected a distinctive radical ideology, drawing on elements of Owenite and Chartist tradition [Tholfsen, 1976]. Thus the transition of nineteenth-century co-operation 'from community-building to shopkeeping' [Pollard, 1960] was by no means sudden or complete. Wider aspirations underlay the struggles of co-operators; indeed their persistence and self-sacrifice under adverse conditions cannot be explained without reference to some element of idealism and collective commitment [Crossick, 1978, chapter 8; Yeo, 1976, *286*]; for example, the political role of the Co-op Women's Guilds from the 1900s cannot be explained in any other terms [Liddington and Norris, 1978, *15*]. There are thus large areas of contradiction and ambiguity in Victorian working-class attitudes, between on the one hand the assertion of working-class identity, on the other the adoption of a consensual language shared with dominant groups in society.

The use of a common language to articulate working-class aspirations could thus conceal a sharp distinction from other sections of society. This ambiguity is apparent in the relationship of the upper strata of the working class and those 'lower-middle-class' groups located socially close to them [see Crossick (ed.), 1977]. Studies of marriage and participation in local organisations reveal a certain amount of contact between skilled workers and white-collar employees and small businessmen [Crossick, 1978, *130–1*; Gray, 1976, *108–11*]. Ideologically there might be an apparently shared commitment to respectability and independence. Many of the lower-middle class groups were also, it seems, recruited from skilled workers or their children. It can thus be argued that 'the boundaries of the labour aristocracy were fluid on one side of its territory' [Hobsbawm, 1964a, *275*]. But there is also evidence of a clear separation from lower-middle-class groups. The social experience of industrial labour and the collective forms of organisation and activity characteristic of skilled workers distinguished them from clerks and small shopkeepers; seeing themselves as the 'great unwashed', the section of society that produces all wealth and gets its hands dirty in the process, working-class people might assert their superiority to 'the "counter-skipper" class' [Wright, 1970, viii]. Trade unionism, whose status generated serious social tensions which threatened the 'mid-Victorian consensus', focused this separate identity. But even those organisations viewed more favourably by bourgeois opinion, such as friendly societies and co-operatives, reflected the collectivism of skilled labour, and had a meaning different from that attributed by middle-class commentators on social improvement. Despite their apparent social proximity to the lower-middle class and their separation from other workers, the upper strata of the working class had a clear sense of class identity.

This identity has to be interpreted in the context of working-class survival in an expanding but unstable capitalist economy [Levitt and Smout, 1979, chapter 6]. The chronic poverty and insecurity of the nineteenth-century subsistence-line is relevant here; even the most 'prosperous' occupational group faced the danger of falling to this level, and their collective organisation and mutual insurance arose from attempts to guard against that danger. Respectable behaviour was related to these problems of survival, and to the self-discipline imposed by the conditions of industrial labour. The respectable behaviour of some sections of the working class, and the growth of institutions underpinning such behaviour was a major preoccupation of contemporary commentators, for instance in debates about parliamentary reform. Such statements have often been taken to indicate the existence of an upper stratum of workers committed to respectability and ripe for 'incorporation' as a subordinate interest in the political nation. But caution is called for in any attempt to relate contemporary identifications of the 'respectable working class' to the concept of labour aristocracy; the two are not interchangeable, whatever complex relationships can be defined between them. For most Victorian social observers, moral evaluations and social distinctions were closely intertwined. References to 'superior' or 'intelligent' artisans thus contain a moral dimension, and do not coincide in any simple way with the boundaries of any particular social stratum. Contemporary terms cannot be assumed to be synonymous with each other, or with such analytical constructs as the historians' labour aristocracy.

Existing studies [including Gray, 1976] have perhaps paid

insufficient attention to these contextual shifts in language and social imagery. As Bailey [1979] has suggested, the scale of nineteenth-century urbanisation, and the invisibility of much working-class life and activity, led observers to abstract out particular aspects of perceived behaviour as bases for social anxiety or reassurance. The growth of saving, home-ownership, and so on was a comforting sign; one witness at the Royal Commission on Friendly Societies attributed the lower crime-rate and diminished need for policing in Birmingham to 'the habits of temperance and frugality engendered and increased by these societies' [Parliamentary Papers, 1871, xxv, q. 3745]. Trade unionism, even in its would-be respectable forms, was less reassuring; while the destruction of machinery and intimidation of non-unionists in Sheffield cutlery and Manchester brickmaking precipitated widespread panics in ruling-class opinion [Price, 1975]. Rioting of a less organised kind by no means disappeared, with Sunday trading riots in 1855, riots at Stalybridge over the administration of relief during the cotton famine, reform riots in 1866, and unemployed riots in 1886–7. At a less dramatic, but more persistent level, the restructuring of leisure did not eradicate such 'unrespectable' activities as heavy social drinking, rowdiness, 'low' entertainments and gambling; it rather altered some of the ground-rules of conflicts over such issues [R. Storch, 'The Problem of Working Class Leisure', in Donajgrodzki (ed.), 1977, 147–55]. Any mid-Victorian consensus around the commitment to respectability and improvement was thus fragile. Even the prolific literature of optimism and social progress may in part have been an attempt to rationalise away deep-rooted fears of a working class that retained its own identity, and its impenetrable cultural defences against middle-class 'improvement'. It is altogether too facile to bracket the resisters neatly as 'plebeians' and the conformists as 'labour aristocrats'.

Inferences from contemporary social stereotyping must therefore be drawn with caution. With the tendency to perceive through stereotypes and the confusion of social and moral categories, Victorian observers could be referring, not to separate social groups, but to the same groups observed in different contexts, subjected to different pressures [see Bailey, 1979]. But, if the boundaries of semi-moral evaluations do not coincide with those of social strata, there may still be a significant overlap. The way in which moral distinctions were linked to income and status at every social level, and the imprecision of the 'fit' between them was a major source of ambiguity and contradiction within Victorian ideology. There is probably some relationship between economic divisions in the working class and images of the 'respectable artisan', but the relationship is a complex one.

6 The Victorian Labour Movement

ONLY small minorities of workers were able to build relatively stable organisations and to impose recognised procedures of collective bargaining in the third quarter of the nineteenth century; and this remained largely true down to the end of the century and beyond, despite waves of unionisation among less skilled groups. The unionised minority was concentrated, as one might expect, among skilled men or others with a measure of job control which they could translate into bargaining-power, often through formal or informal restrictions on recruitment. Apart from the apprenticed skilled trades in building, engineering and urban crafts, these included hewers in the better-organised coalfields, and spinners in cotton. It is important to bear in mind here that groups described as 'strong' were so relative to the extreme weakness of other groups, just as economic 'prosperity' was relative to the abysmal poverty of most workers. Destruction of union organisation by systematic victimisation and lock-out, leaving many firms 'closed' to unionists for years afterwards, could easily occur even in the best-organised trades; such experiences were central to the class consciousness of skilled labour.

The concept of labour aristocracy has perhaps been most useful in drawing attention to the narrow base of the Victorian unions, and their adoption in many cases of strategies and models of organisation of limited applicability to those less advantageously placed in the labour market. This could go along with social complacency, indifference to the problems of less organised groups, combined with contempt for their failure to organise, and a refusal to envisage forms of organisation that did not conform to established institutional models. Frustration at these characteristics – often on the part of younger men who, like Tom Mann, themselves belonged to craft unions – underlay polemical uses of the term 'labour aristocracy' in the early socialist movement, from where it subsequently passed into Marxist theory and historiography [Field, 1978 – 9, *66*]. Attempts to extend the **boundaries of trade unionism involved a redefinition of its terms of** of reference; as the Edinburgh socialist newspaper argued in 1895:

When we speak of a trade we mean not only those workers who have served an apprenticeship to any given occupation to the exclusion of those whose occupations require comparatively little skill, but rather the word in its broader sense, by which . . . we mean all the workers who earn their bread by the exercise of one particular calling [quoted in Gray, 1976, *170*].

The very term 'trades unions', suggesting an amalgam of sectional groups, is perhaps a revealing indication of the character of the British labour movement.

These features of exclusivity and sectionalism are often identified with the Webbs' 'new model' [Webb, 1920, chapter 4], and the thesis of some kind of watershed in trade union history around the late 1840s and early 50s. The Webbs emphasised the emergence of large, centralised craft amalgamated societies, pursuing limited and conciliatory aims; they saw this as following the failure of broader-based but 'utopian' movements such as Owenism, and the defeat of aspirations for radical political change. More recent historians have pointed out that the adoption of 'new model' methods was not universal, and that their significance (especially as regards industrial 'pacifism' and the role of welfare benefits provided by unions) can be misunderstood. As Cole [1962] notes, a number of important unions in mining and cotton had a broader industrial base (although their practice might well take on craft-like features, representing particularly a limited section of the labour force); several of the crafts developed federal forms more decentralised than those implied by the 'new model' (as, for example, in printing: see Child [1967]). Even within the major amalgamated societies themselves, there were tensions between London-based leaders and provincial branches and districts.

Industrial 'pacifism' and an emphasis on welfare benefits and the search for legitimacy have been seen as characteristics of the 'new model' craft unions – often, originally, by frustrated militants within those unions. While such tendencies did develop, they must be interpreted in the light of the structure and practices of Victorian trade unionism. . Craft union activity often took the form of 'regulation by union rule' [Child, 1967, part III], a day-to-day struggle in the workshop to uphold trade custom as the defence against methods of intensified exploitation [for examples, see Gray, 1976, *147–8*; Jeffreys, 1945, *101–3*]. Branches retained a good deal of autonomy in acting to defend *existing* wages and conditions, which were locally determined. It was at points where such local conflicts threatened to escalate into a wider confrontation, or where branches initiated 'forward' movements, that the executives sought to exercise control [Murphy, 1978]. Union rules restricting the power to initiate strike action have to be seen in this wider context. Despite such rules, local campaigns over wages and hours could emerge in defiance of executive instructions, like the nine hours' movement in the north east of England in 1871 [Allen, 1971]. The provision of welfare benefits cannot be seen simply as a diversion from the unions' industrial function; they kept sick and unemployed men off the labour market, and provided a means of sanctioning recalcitrant members [Child, 1967, *124–32*]. Although 'provident' aspects were a major issue at the 1867 Royal Commission on Trade Unions, the industrial aspects were by no means obscured; the working of the welfare side was itself dependent on a background of occupational culture and industrial solidarity [Thane, 1976]. When challenged by the 'orthodox' economic argument that unions interfered with individual bargaining in the marketplace, Applegarth defended the right of the collectivity to make rules: 'if we are all to be left to do as we like the sooner we dissolve our society the better', and to impose 'a fair day's work for a fair day's wage' [Royal Commission on Trade Unions, 1867]. Cautious and respectable leaders thus always recognised that in the last analysis the workers' position could only be protected by collective action; such slogans as 'a fair day's wage' reflected an instinctive resistance to ruling-class ideas.

The picture of mid-Victorian trade unionism is thus more complicated than monolithic domination by centralised, exclusive and cautious craft amalgamated societies. Organisational forms were more diverse than that, and there were important tensions within the 'new model' societies themselves. It is true, however, that the unions were characterised by their narrow basis, even in industries without formal skill qualifications. The emergence of stable organisation in the most powerful sections of the working class, and the establishment of collective bargaining procedures at local level helped institutionalise the separate position of the more organised groups [Burgess, 1975]. It is an over-simplification to see this merely in terms of the 'incorporation' of a labour aristocracy into the existing society, or of collaboration between union leaders and employers. Although it is possible to identify tendencies of this sort, they were always liable to reversal and subject to challenge within the unions themselves. The conservatism of many mid-Victorian union leaders reflected the hardening of a tactical response into a rule of conduct which could, in different situations, become inappropriate. Conciliation agreements, for instance, arose where 'the unions had sufficient strength to convince the employers that conciliation and arbitration were necessary, but insufficient power to make an openly militant policy more attractive', and broke down when the balance of forces shifted [Porter, 1970]. Attempts to assert central leadership and limit rank-and-file initiative in some respects reflected the weakness of unions, the difficulty of maintaining their cohesion and institutional existence, and the dangers of local activity sparking off wider confrontations in unfavourable circumstances.

The relationship of militancy to tactical caution on one hand, and a wider ideological accommodation to capitalist power on the other raises problems of leadership and organisational structure that are not specific to craft unions, or to the nineteenth century. If trade unionism can be identified with rather limited sections of the working class this does not imply that the views of leaders were necessarily the views of that stratum [cf. Moorhouse, 1978, *80*], although there is undoubtedly some kind of relationship between them. Nor do advocates of more militant policies in particular situations necessarily represent a different section of the working class or an alternative conception of the labour movement's goals and strategy. George Potter, the critic of Applegarth and the other amalgamated society leaders, shared many of their social and political attitudes [Burgess, 1975, *103*]. Rank-and-file militancy could be more intensely sectional than the leaders, for example over demarcation issues [Melling, 1980; Robertson, 1975]. With the growth of socialism from the 1880s, on the other hand, immediate demands for more militant and forward-looking policies could sometimes be linked to an alternative industrial and political vision.

The importance of craft control on the job meant that skilled trade unionists were often divided, not just from the unskilled, but also against each other [Reid, 1978, *358 – 9*]. Such sectionalism can be found throughout the history of the working class. It has been argued, for example, that the 'new model' unions and the separation off of 'aristocratic' trades shows a basic continuity from the second to the third quarters of the nineteenth century; there was no mid-century turning-point, but a steady development of more adequate forms of craft union organisation [see Musson, 1962]. But such generalisations can obscure the peculiar features of specific periods; a continuous institutional existence has to be interpreted in the light of changes in the wider context within which the institutions operated.

> What was new was surely the dominance of such groups in the labour movement. Primacy in the third quarter of the century lay with them, but perhaps the preceding one belonged to weavers, other outworkers, and lower artisans, many of them, like shoemakers and tailors, declining . . . [Prothero, 1971, *205 – 6*].

The third quarter of the nineteenth century is distinguished by the greater stability of craft unions based on the better trades, their adaptation to larger-scale production and labour mobility. The struggle to legalise union activity, and to achieve a wider recognition of the working class presence in the community fostered a common sense of identity among these skilled trades. The formation of local Trades Councils in the big cities and later of the TUC were institutional expressions of this; such bodies often originated in campaigns for the reform of contract and trade union law [Fraser, 1974, *45 – 52*, chapter 8; MacDougal (ed.), 1968]. If the identity of trade unionists was narrowly based, it still reflected some common interests beyond immediate craft sectionalism. As at other times in the history of the movement, there was an uneasy co-existence of sectional and broader types of activity.

Changes in the nature of working-class politics have been one theme in historiographical uses of the concept of labour aristocracy. Such uses postulate a shift about the mid-century towards greater accommodation to the established framework of capitalist society, and relate this shift to the emergence of the upper stratum. Contrasts between the militancy of the Chartist years and mid-Victorian quiescence can be over-drawn, to the neglect of important chronological and regional differences in the various processes which together made for grater social stability. Traditions of popular radicalism persisted and, far from being suppressed by mid-Victorian Liberalism, helped shape it [Tholfsen, 1976]. But the context of popular politics changed, in ways analogous to changes in such organisations as friendly societies, co-operatives and trade unions. There was more room for accommodation and negotiation, scope for the pursuit of limited goals, and less capacity to mobilise broad-based popular movements around radical demands. The reform of the franchise in 1867 was not followed by the dramatic working-class entry into politics some contemporaries had feared [see Harrison, 1965]. But working-class support for the Liberal Party, which was the predominant but not universal allegiance of the more organised parts of the working class, involved tensions over claims to stronger representation of labour within the Liberal framework and such issues as trade union law. But dissidence over candidatures or specific policy questions was not sustained by any ideological critique of Liberal-Radicalism until the emergence of socialism in the 1880s. Like other working-class attitudes, support for established political parties involved an ambiguous relationship between the self-assertion of 'labour' as a distinct, at times aggressive, interest within a broader community consensus, and acceptance of ruling-class leadership. In some places, particularly the cotton towns, there is evidence of employer influence on political affiliations [Joyce, 1975]; but even in such cases employers' strategies and rhetorical appeals may have been adapted to the irremovable presence of an organised and articulate working class [Foster, 1974, chapter 7]. Mid-Victorian 'consensus' arose from ruling-class attempts to come to terms with the lessons of the Chartist experience, not from a simple suppression of that experience. Thus Vincent [1966] has argued that working-class Liberalism can only be understood in terms of the popular roots and internal diversity of the Gladstonian Liberal Party.

Some elements of the labour movement began to challenge the limits of the Liberal tradition from the 1880s, with attempts to build broader labour organisations, the ideological challenge of socialism, and stronger political self-assertion. Such developments have been related, not just to the unionisation of less skilled groups – which was often ephemeral in character [Clegg, Fox and Thompson, 1964, chapter 2] – but also to changes in the skilled trades. The industrial climate became less favourable and conflicts over manning, demarcation and working practices intensified, especially in engineering [Jeffreys, 1945, *121 – 44*]. The early socialist organisations attracted considerable support from skilled workers [Gray, 1976, chapter 9; Hopkin, 1975; Pelling, 1968, *58 – 9*]. At the same time, new industrial pressures, organised strike-breaking activities and adverse legal judgements created wider interest in independent labour politics in the 1890s and 1900s. This trend was reinforced by the inflexible response of Liberal organisations to demands for labour representation. The new developments were thus as much the result of changes in the outlook and activities of previously organised groups as of the spread of trade unionism to the hitherto unorganised.

It has been argued, on rather more fragmentary evidence, that changes in urban communities, including notably the social impact of the expanding white-collar strata, made for greater cultural homogeneity among manual workers and a sharper separation from the rest of society [Gray, 1976, *115 – 20, 169*]. For whatever reasons – and the simple availability of new ideas should not be under-estimated as a factor – labour politics was beginning to change in the 1880s and 90s.

7 Imperialism and the British Working Class

THE preceding chapters have reviewed evidence of social distinctions in the Victorian working class and their consequences for relationships between classes and the development of labour organisations. The labour aristocracy debate has also raised some broader questions of historical interpretation, which will be considered in this and the following chapter.

For Engels, the phenomena he observed and deplored were transient effects of Britain's industrial lead and monopolisation of the world market in manufactured goods: 'And that is the reason why, since the dying-out of Owenism, there has been no Socialism in England' [Marx and Engels, 1962 edn, *31*]. While Engels was perhaps rather mechanistic in seeing a revival of socialism as the necessary consequence of the erosion of British industrial superiority, his analysis of the impact of British industrial supremacy in the third quarter of the nineteenth century has been confirmed by subsequent studies. In the key engineering industry, the opening up of export markets eased the pressure on employers, creating room for wage bargaining and the maintenance of craft control over work methods [Burgess, 1975, *4*]. The expansion of the capital goods sector and the process of urban growth, both involving much skill-intensive investment and employment, underpinned the 'mid-Victorian boom'. In this situation there was greater margin for conceding wage-increases, and less pressure on employers to rationalise the methods of production. Some, mostly skilled and almost exclusively adult male, sections of the labour force were better able than others to benefit from these conditions.

Lenin's analysis is rather different. He was concerned with such late-nineteenth- and twentieth-century developments as the Boer War, great power conflicts in the Balkans and the origins of the First World War on the one hand; on the other, with the failure of socialist and labour movements effectively to oppose the imperialist activities of their national states, culminating in many cases in enthusiastic participation in the war effort. He saw these political attitudes as exemplifying opportunist 'social chauvinism' in the working-class movement linked to the formation of 'privileged sections . . . among the workers' [Lenin, 1968 edn, *246*]. The continuing debate, among Marxist scholars as much as among critics of Marxism, about Lenin's analysis of imperialism cannot adequately be discussed here. With reference to British experience, it has been pointed out that there was no clear correlation between imperial expansion and the destination of overseas investment; British industrial and financial interests continued to depend on free trade, often creating what would nowadays be termed 'neo-colonial' relationships to formally independent countries in other parts of the world [Barratt Brown, 1970]. While this role in the world economy, and the support to the balance of payments from returns on overseas investment certainly created an environment in which there was some leeway for organised labour, the connection between imperialism and higher living-standards is a complex one; given the separation of finance from industry, it is unclear how Lenin's 'bribe' to the labour aristocracy got from the City to industrial labour [see Field, 1978 – 9, *72*]. Indeed to talk, even polemically, of the 'bribery' of strata of the labour force suggests an extraordinary degree of conspiratorial premeditation. But these criticisms of Lenin aside, there may still be significant connections between British imperialism, economic relationships to the future 'third world', and the environment within which workers were able to make gains.

Foster [1974, *203 – 4, 250*] projects Lenin's account of late-nineteenth-century 'new imperialism' backwards to the 1850s, partly assimilating it to Engels's remarks about industrial monopoly. Foster thus emphasises the role of 'capital-export imperialism' in the mid-century stabilisation of the economy and class relations. The export of British capital was certainly a major element in the mid-Victorian economic expansion; and most historians seem agreed that this occurred in a kind of symbiotic relationship to industry, creating markets for the key capital goods sector. But the connections of this to imperial expansion are obscure. Whatever the value of Lenin's analysis of the 'new imperialism' of the scramble for Africa and subsequent events, the mid-nineteenth-century British empire was a rather different form of imperialism demanding separate analysis. The mid-Victorian period, often seen as the 'classical period of the . . . labour aristocracy' [Hobsbawm, 1964*a*, *272*], thus represents an earlier phase of capitalist development from that described in Lenin's use of the concept. Foster also follows Lenin in leaving unspecified the links between different sectors, through which any gains from imperialism and overseas investment would presumably have to be distributed.

The postulated relationship between imperialism and the development of the working class raises ideological as well as economic problems. Lenin's central concern was with the failure of international socialism in the crisis of the war. He related this to the implantation of 'chauvinism' in a working class corrupted by imperialism, whose upper strata were especially susceptible to this process, and the consequent complicity of labour organisations in the imperialist ambitions of 'their' governments. Recent studies suggest that there is little evidence for positive working-class interest in, or enthusiasm for, the empire. As Price [1972] shows, enlistment during the Boer War reflected the trade cycle, the imperial issue was not decisive in the Conservative election victory of 1900, and 'jingo' crowds were composed of young white-collar workers and students rather than of manual workers [see also Pelling, 1968, chapter 5]. Although 'social imperialism', or attempts to mitigate class tensions by imperial ideology and economic strategies based on empire, was a significant trend of political opinion in the 1900s, ranging from Conservatives and Unionists to some Fabian socialists [Semmel, 1960], it was by no means dominant; it was opposed by some elements of the mainstream Liberal tradition, by radical intellectuals (some of whom, like Hobson, argued a 'social anti-imperialism' suggesting that imperialist policies benefited a parasitic élite to the detriment of industrial expansion at home and the living-standards of British workers), and by many strands of labour and socialist opinion. In so far as interests and attitudes varied within the working class, distinctions between industrial sectors may be more helpful than 'horizontal' divisions between labour aristocrats and others [Gupta, 1975, *3–4*]. There is therefore little or no evidence of strong working-class commitment to imperialist policies, or of differences in attitude between strata of the working class. But this does not resolve the matter. Indifferent or even critical attitudes to empire and opposition to particular imperial adventures could be quite compatible with a deeper sense of national superiority and complicity in the maintenance of British imperial supremacy – whose lynchpins, Ireland and India, had after all been acquired long before the 'new imperialism' of the late- nineteenth century. The general socialist attitude of 'abhorrence of colonial wars, a condescending attitude to non-European civilisations and an implicit assumption of leadership' [Gupta, 1975, 8] could certainly fall within the bounds of what Lenin termed 'chauvinism'.[7]

Chauvinist attitudes could also be expressed in responses to immigrant workers [see Lunn (ed.), 1980]. Ethnic origin, sometimes compounded by religion, provided one basis for control over labour recruitment and sectional bargaining strategies. Unionism in the Lanark coalfield became tinged with Orangism in a period of weakness and retreat during the 1860s [Campbell in Harrison (ed.), 1978]. The Orange movement was also an important base of support for popular Toryism in Lancashire [N. Kirk, 'Class, Ethnicity and Popular Toryism', in Lunn (ed.), 1980]. Tensions may have been greatest in the poorest and least organised sections of the working class, possibly because the issue of immigrants entering more tightly organised trades did not arise in the first place. Campaigns against sweating sometimes contained an anti-Semitic element, identifying sweaters with 'Jews'. There were repeated trade union calls for control over the entry of 'alien' labour, despite the reversal of the 1892 TUC resolution to that effect; but there were inhibitions on the articulation of such demands in racist terms. It is difficult to assess how far racist sentiments were latent in the working class in a diffuse form, and how far attitudes differed in different strata.

There is also evidence of institutionalised patriotic if not necessarily imperialist or chauvinist sentiment in the Victorian working class. A network of voluntary associations, some with semi-official state backing, from the rifle volunteers to the boys' brigade and boy scouts sought to foster such values [Summers, 1976]. This can be viewed in terms of 'social imperialist' efforts by ruling-class groups, or crudely manipulative models of social control. But the origins of these activities are more complex. The rifle volunteers began in 1859 as a spontaneous movement, attracting widespread support from skilled workers and viewed with some suspicion by the military establishment [Cunningham, 1976]. Such movements exemplify the self-assertive demand for citizenship rights and a recognised status in the community characteristic of mid-Victorian working-class radicalism. However it may ultimately have lent itself to strategies of 'incorporation', this self-assertion could generate tensions; there were even fears about the wisdom of issuing arms to working-class civilians.

Support for these movements no doubt reflected a variety of motives, including purely recreational ones, but their patriotic aspect cannot be seen simply as the product of élite manipulation. [8] Popular patriotism related back to the tradition of the 'freeborn Englishman' and its Scottish counterparts, an assertion of political rights within the nation as well as of allegiance to it. When Bronterre O'Brien, the old Chartist leader, attacked the Crimean War in Oldham a local radical took issue with him:

> Mr O'Brien had told them that their conditions were as bad or worse than Russian serfs, but he would ask him to point to a page in history where Russian serfs could meet and discuss public questions as they were doing that night (hear, hear and cheers) – where Russian serfs could eat white bread and good and wholesome food [Quoted in Foster, 1974, *242*].

Enthusiasm for British military exploits was based on identification with the courage and endurance of the ordinary soldier – and often involved criticisms of the unreformed army system. The relationship of this popular tradition to a more aggressive sense of national superiority and an expansionist imperialism is complex and needs fuller study. That governments could draw on it to support their policies was shown in the Boer War (the volunteer regiments' baptism of fire) and, more completely, in 1914 and after. The 'pals' battalions' at the Somme, recruited by occupational and cultural affiliation, are reminiscent of Victorian traditions of voluntary effort and civic participation, shared by the working class as well as other sections of society. [9]

8 The Stability of Capitalist Society

THE labour aristocracy is often seen as playing a crucial role in the attainment of a measure of social stability about the middle of the nineteenth century or, more widely, in explaining the 'gradualist' characteristics of the British labour movement. The third quarter of the nineteenth century has interested historians as a period when the British ruling class, in contrast to its counterparts elsewhere, learnt to live with independent working-class organisations and opinions, to rule through negotiation and concession. It is however important to note that, contrary to crudely manipulative theories of the 'incorporation' of the working class, this way of ruling was imposed by working-class resistance during the Chartist period and after on a ruling class that itself had to undergo changes in coming to terms with the 'working-class presence'. There were continuing social tensions and an ever-present threat of the escalation of conflict; 'consensus' was always precarious, its terms subject to redefinition and re-negotiation.

The attainment of this equilibrium was a complex process, and historians who emphasise the emergence of the labour aristocracy would not necessarily suggest that it was the only or the most important factor [Crossick, 1978, *15 – 16*]. Most treatments of the labour aristocracy theme in fact describe various effects within the working class of wider changes in the economy, class relationships, politics and the state. The greater economic stability and underlying buoyancy of the mid-Victorian boom was certainly a crucial element; it widened the margin for bargaining between employers and workers, and induced a general atmosphere of social optimism and expansion. But social stability did not follow automatically from economic changes. Those changes were in any case neither immediate nor evenly spread over industries and regions, and it is only with hindsight that the late 1840s and 50s can be seen as a turning-point.

The nature of economic development, the importance of craft skills in key sectors and the general experience of an expanding and relatively stable capitalist economy had profound fragmenting effects on the working class. The various definitions of the labour aristocracy all refer to the responses of narrowly based well-organised groups to that general situation. But it had effects on all strata of the working class and sex, regional differences, ethnic and religious divisions were all factors in the process of subdivision. Such groups as the Black Country nailmakers or the East End clothing trades, whose living-standards made little or no advance, perhaps found themselves isolated and without hope, cut off from the organised and advancing sections of the working class.

Stabilisation also had political dimensions. Foster [1974], for example, rightly emphasises the significance of changes within the ruling class and in its strategies towards other classes. The crisis years of the 1830s and 40s had been marked by deep divisions among the dominant groups in society; these divisions of interest and ideology certainly persisted, but with political reforms and a more buoyant economic climate they could be expressed within a wider consensus. Consensus within the state – or rather a balance of competing interests – facilitated the development of institutions of coercion and control, adapted to new urban conditions. The eventual imposition of poor law reform and police forces represented an important coercive element in the stability of Victorian society. Working-class moral conformity could reflect the sanctions of police, elementary school, poor law and charity in the community, and the demands of adaptation to the work-disciplines of a system whose continued existence seemed assured in the work-place [see Donajgrodzki (ed.), 1977; Foster, 1974; Storch, 1975].

Alongside this framework of coercive control there were important elements of voluntary consent to the existing structure of society. The ruling class itself was not monolithic; diversity and pluralism and the consequent emphasis on competing voluntary institutions was indeed a source of strength in maintaining bourgeois leadership in urban society [see Morris, 1977, *62 – 3*]. The middle layers in society, composed of small shopkeepers and tradesmen, clerks and so on, played an important role in this process [Crossick (ed.), 1977; Foster, 1974, *166 – 77*]. Social stability did not depend simply on the imposition of a single ruling-class ideology, but on the building of a consensus among a number of competing tendencies. Ruling-class ideologies were themselves transformed with the 'mellowing of Liberalism' [Tholfsen, 1976, chapter 4] to incorporate and emasculate elements of the popular radical tradition. In Oldham the popular leaders of the Chartist period 'can be found continuing their activity *inside* the new Tory and Liberal parties . . . it was the continued identification of these two groupings with their original slogans which enabled the two parties to win mass support' [Foster, 1974, *209 – 10*]. This created a kind of limited and indirect working-class political representation even before 1867.

Discussions about the labour aristocracy belong in the context of this complex process of economic change and political accommodation. Whatever the ultimate value of the concept, it does point to the important fact that labour organisation was relatively narrowly based, and subjected to these pressures of 'incorporation'. That working-class organisation and political consciousness should develop unevenly, and develop most strongly among those in relatively good positions is in itself not surprising, or peculiar to the second half of the nineteenth century. But historical questions remain about the extent to which such better-organised groups were insulated from the experience of those in weaker positions. This varies at different periods, and historians who contrast the second and third quarters of the nineteenth century are drawing attention to such variations. Whereas many sectors of the working class felt threatened, potentially if not actually, by new forms of exploitation during the second quarter, the stronger groups managed to re-stabilise their position in the later period. Prothero [1971] has shown the prominence of sweated trades in London Chartism. Political institutions and ideologies also played a role in encouraging more 'open' or 'closed' forms of working-class action. The identity of the working class or of 'labour' at particular periods was defined in terms of language, social imagery and modes of political rhetoric. Chartism and Owenism in the 1830s and 40s were arguably more 'open' and inclusive, while the language of trade unionism and radicalism in the third quarter of the century was more restricted in its appeals. Unionism, whose relative importance increased, was defined as the attribute of those with a 'trade'; Campbell [in Harrison (ed.) 1978, *94*] has shown how the ideology of the Scots 'independent collier', drawing on Burns and other native cultural resources, reinforced the exclusion of the Irish, and perpetuated models of trade unionism inappropriate for large sectors of the labour fource. The implicit assumption that the working class consists of adult males is perhaps the commonest and deepest-rooted linguistic exclusion of the experience of other groups, and one by no means confined to the period under discussion.

The concept of labour aristocracy at least helped draw attention to these tendencies. It has also been deployed more broadly, in attempts to explain the distinctive features of the British labour movement [see for example Gray, 1976, chapter 10]. The second half of the nineteenth century is seen as a formative period in labour history, with the development of more stable organisation, the extension of political rights, and the beginning by the end of the century of independent labour politics. The socialist-trade-union alliance in the formation of the Labour Party, and the eclectic character of its political theory, are interpreted in terms of the changing position and outlook of the late-Victorian labour aristocracy. The limited political horizons of the working class are thus seen as a historical inheritance from these developments. One difficulty of such interpretations is that they can lead to a view of subsequent history as predetermined at some single formative moment. This view assumes moreover that the ideology of the labour aristocracy was somehow diffused to the rest of the working class, rather as some accounts of the labour aristocracy itself assume a rather simple downward transmission of bourgeois ideologies [cf. Moorhouse, 1978].

Emphasis on the role of the Victorian labour aristocracy should not therefore be allowed to foreshorten analysis of subsequent periods and other strata of the working class. But ideological and organisational traditions derived from earlier experiences do play some part in the development of labour movements [cf. Hobsbawm, 1964a, chapter 18], and the gradualism and theoretical eclecticism of the British movement can be related, among other things, to traditions derived from the mid- and late-nineteenth century.

For the workers, having failed to overthrow capitalist society, proceeded to warren it from end to end . . . Each assertion of working-class influence within the bourgeois-democratic state machinery, simultaneously involved them as partners (even if antagonistic partners) in the running of the machine [Thompson, 1978, 71].

This process began earlier and developed further in Britain than elsewhere. Against this emphasis on national peculiarities, it has been argued that 'the outcome of the capital/labour conflict in a wide range of capitalist countries seventy-five to one hundred years later has been remarkably similar' [Moorhouse, 1978, *81*]. This may possibly be true, in the sense that the economic and political power of capital remains intact; but that somewhat tautologous statement should not be allowed to obscure the significant historical and national differences in the political cohesion and militancy of the working class, and the extent to which capitalist power is surrounded by an effective political and ideological consensus. For the historian, it is such differences that are of interest. It can scarcely be denied that the histories of the main European countries are very different, producing inherited national traditions of labour and socialist politics.

International comparisons can thus shed some light on the relative stability of British society and the role played by particular groups of the working class. French and Italian skilled workers seem to have played a leading role in nineteenth-century labour movements comparable to their counterparts in Britain [Moss, 1976; Bell, 1978]; indeed the craft basis of the movement was possibly more pronounced, given the lower level of development of factory industry in these countries. Scott's [1974] study of the Carmaux glass-workers also suggests interesting parallels in the turn to socialism and a broader class politics of previously isolated skilled groups feeling the impact of intensified industrial pressures in the 1890s. Given the similarity in occupational make-up, it could be argued that the undoubted differences in political attitude and experience simply reflected national cultures and an inherited rhetoric and social imagery; or that the rhetoric was in fact a thin veneer covering essentially similar political practices [Moorhouse, 1978, *81*]. The elements of tradition are clearly important. But there may equally be differences in the economic and social position of apparently similar occupational groups; skilled labour might have rather different experiences in different countries. For a number of economic and political reasons, there was more room for concession and negotiation in the British situation. Moss [1976, *15*] suggests that French skilled workers did not enjoy improvements in real wages comparable to their British counterparts; they may thus have been more aware of the situation and demands of less organised and articulate strata of the working class (the surfacing of these demands, for example among working-class women, was a notable feature of the Paris Commune). The harshly and overtly repressive face of the state in most European countries was another important factor, one index of this being the illegality for long periods of workers' movements. To argue about the primacy of political tradition, economic situation or state repression is of limited value. These elements were mutually reinforcing, within a total situation that contrasts at a number of points with that in Britain. The labour aristocracy thesis thus raises broader questions about the distinctive features of British labour history, even if it cannot entirely resolve them.

9 Conclusions

AS even its critics recognise, the concept of labour aristocracy 'has had its value in drawing attention to differences within the working class' [Pelling, 1968, *61*]. Debate has centred round the specific form of these differences in the second half of the nineteenth century, and the validity of generalising across a range of industries and communities. The concept may sometimes lead historians to force a variety of situations to fit a single model, or to expand the model so that it loses in precision and explanatory power what it gains in empirical relevance. The influence of the concept has also led to neglect of other bases of social division, notably that between the sexes, which cannot be discussed purely in terms of occupational structures.

More positively, the labour aristocracy thesis has helped historians to get beyond a view of the working class as a homogeneous entity, and encouraged them to investigate the experience and activity of different groups. This has revealed much evidence of the tendency for stronger groups of workers, better placed to take advantage of the mid-Victorian boom, to pull apart from weaker groups. As critics have pointed out, however, it does not necessarily follow that these stronger groups can all be seen as occupying a common social position and forming a coherent social stratum; their advantaged situation might be relatively transient, depending on personal strength and efficiency which declined with age, and their relations to the less advantaged might be mediated by kinship and the sexual and generational division of labour. But the labour aristocracy thesis has been of value in directing attention to the tendency for groups to pull apart and to experience the general economic expansion of the period in different ways. This has been important as a corrective to loose generalisations about economic prosperity and the integration of the working class into capitalist society. The image of increasing prosperity was most convincingly based on such groups as the skilled engineering and building workers, some hewers in mining, cotton spinners, and so on; casual dock labour, the sweated trades, women's employment generally, the casualised sections of skilled labour give a very different perspective on the alleged filtering down of Victorian business prosperity.

The strongest evidence for the formation of a distinct upper stratum of the working class comes from trades like engineering, building and such urban crafts as printing, characterised by an apprenticeship system and a sharp distinction between members and non-members of 'the trade'. The largest concentrations of these groups were in large, occupationally heterogeneous urban centres; urban institutions, including those of organised labour, helped foster a common sense of identity. The most useful conception of the labour aristocracy may after all be one of the earliest, that of Friedrich Engels, who emphasised 'the labour of *grown-up men*' and 'the great Trades' Unions'.

The most fruitful application of the concept is perhaps to an examination of the Victorian labour movement, with its rather limited occupational bases and characteristic pattern of piecemeal advance. The large urban centres, in which it seems easiest to identify a distinct upper stratum, had a wider influence on the world of organised labour, being for instance the first places to establish Trades Councils. And the values, organisational methods and strategies of Victorian trade unionism reflected this influence in a wider range of occupational groups. While it may be misleading to identify a comparable social stratum in many industries and communities, the tendencies of behaviour and values to which studies of the labour aristocracy have drawn attention cannot be overlooked. Even if historians conclude that the concept should in the end be abandoned, they should beware of throwing out the baby with the bath-water. Both contemporary and historiographic uses refer to real historical processes, however unsatisfactorily they describe and explain those processes.

The discussion around the labour aristocracy has inevitably raised far wider themes, touching on such fundamental problems as the periodisation of British social development and the thesis of a transition to a more stable capitalist society after about 1850. Rather than continue to argue about alternative definitions of the labour aristocracy and whether or not such a social group existed, it may be more fruitful, at this stage of the debate, to explore these wider problems. It therefore seems appropriate, by way of conclusion, to indicate some of the major themes and areas for research and discussion that have emerged from the preceding pages [cf. Field, 1978 – 9, who reaches rather similar conclusions].

First, there is scope for investigation of technology, work organisation and production processes in different industries. The persistence of craft methods, often within mechanised processes, and the importance of subdivision and the degradation of skilled labour in workshop and domestic trades pose important questions. The very definitions of labour as 'skilled' or 'unskilled' cannot be taken at face value. The job control of different groups, and their ability to regulate occupational recruitment are key aspects, to which formally defined skill may be more or less relevant.

Second, the relationship of sexual divisions to occupational hierarchies. Feminist historians have made us aware of the limitations of implicitly adult male definitions of the working class. In many industries the 'aristocrats' were men and the 'plebeians' women. This belongs in the wider context of the subordination of women to men at all social levels, and the burden of female household labour. Differences in the exact form and boundaries of the sexual division of labour, and its relationship to occupation and employment conditions need fuller study.

Third, problems of language and social imagery are relevant in a number of ways to the analysis of the working class, for instance in interpreting comments on the 'superior artisan' or 'respectable working man'. It is necessary for historians to pay closer attention to contextual shifts in meaning, and possible ambiguities in the social imagery available to different groups.

Fourth, behaviour outside work, and the whole pattern of working-class 'respectability' has to be more closely related to changes in the labour process, work-discipline and adaptation to the conditions of labour. Closer investigation of the impact of such developments on different groups may call into question any simple equation of respectability with a labour aristocracy.

Fifth, one direction of recent work has been to raise questions about developments in the ruling class and the institutions of the state, as they affected the working class. Labour historians have often made implicit assumptions about a monolithic ruling class whose identity is static and unambiguous (or at most subdivided between landed and urban industrial interests). But in any specific situation workers confronted this employer, that magistrate, or that professional expert — not the ruling class as a whole. There could be more or less wide divergences in the interests and values of these various categories. While intellectuals concerned to achieve class conciliation might welcome the emergence of high-paid groups of skilled workers, employers might look for ways to cut their wages and break their areas of control in the workshop. The shifting balance between such interests, and the support they found in society as a whole had a considerable impact on the situation confronting working people and their institutions.

Sixth and finally, many arguments about the labour aristocracy centre round implied comparisons between Britain and other capitalist societies. Systematic comparative studies are needed, to establish the nature and significance of national differences in the development of the working class. National political traditions, economic conditions and the structures of the state are all relevant factors. Their inter-relations need to be better understood.

If the labour aristocracy debate serves to stimulate further study of these key problems, it will have proved valuable in posing historical questions if not necessarily in answering them satisfactorily.

Notes and References

(The place of publication is London unless otherwise stated.)

1. See A. Gramsci, *Selections from Prison Notebooks* (1971); for a critique of mechanistic Marxism, see especially pp. 158–85.
2. See for example R. Blackburn (ed.), *Ideology in Social Science* (1972); J. H. Goldthorpe *et al.*, *The Affluent Worker in the Class Structure* (Cambridge, 1969).
3. D. N. Paton *et al.*, *A Study of the Diet of the Labouring Classes in the City of Edinburgh* (Edinburgh, *c.* 1900) p. 30.
4. I am indebted to J. Woodhurst for allowing me to read as yet unpublished research investigating these crucial problems.
5. See M. Weber, 'Class, Status and Party', in H. H. Gerth and C. Wright Mills (eds), *From Max Weber: Essays in Sociology* (1948). It should be noted that Weber did not simply add a qualification to Marx's emphasis on class conflict, but also defined class in a different and in some ways *more* narrowly 'economic' sense. Reid [1978, *356* footnote] interestingly suggests 'Weberian' elements in Crossick [1978] and Gray [1976]; but a recognition of the phenomena to which Weber drew attention does not imply any necessary commitment to his conceptualisation of them – it could for instance contribute to a more complex and flexible understanding of a Marxian concept of class struggle. These theoretical issues are outside our present scope, but for recent Marxist discussion on class see Judith Bloomfield, 'Marxist Writing on Class', *Marxism Today* (October 1978); and A. Hunt (ed.), *Class and Class Structure* (1977).
6. This criticism is probably more applicable to some of Weber's self-styled disciples than to Weber himself; if Marx has suffered mechanistic distortion at the hands of 'vulgar Marxists' Weber has met an analogous fate in academic sociology.

7. For the impact of Lenin's ideas in creating greater awareness of colonial issues, see S. MacIntyre, *Imperialism and the British Labour Movement in the 1920s* (Our History pamphlet no. 64, Communist Party History Group, 1975).

8. G. Eley, 'Defining Social Imperialism', *Social History*, no. 3 (1976) similarly criticises manipulative analyses of lower-middle-class participation in patriotic movements in Germany.

9. See J. Keegan, *The Face of Battle* (Harmondsworth: Penguin edn, 1978), pp. 221–4.

Bibliography

SECTION I: SOURCE MATERIALS

A range of source material for nineteenth-century working-class history is available in recent reprints and collections. The following selection is intended to indicate the main types of source used by historians.

Booth, Charles, *Life and Labour of the People of London* (5 vols, 1969; reprint of 1902 edn). This massive survey (much of it in fact by Booth's associates, including Beatrice Potter, the future Beatrice Webb) is sooner or later consulted by every student of the period.

Burnett, J. (ed.), *Useful Toil: Autobiographies of Working People from the 1820s to the 1920s* (1974). Includes recently discovered manuscripts as well as reprinting excerpts from some better-known autobiographies.

Cole, G. D. H., and Filson, A. W. (eds), *British Working Class Movements: Select Documents, 1787–1875* (1951). A standard collection covering main developments in trade unions, co-operatives, radicalism, and so on.

Gorman, J., *Banner Bright* (1973). Generously illustrated study of trade union banners, showing their value for the study of attitudes and social imagery; particularly good on mid-Victorian craft ideologies.

MacDougall, I. (ed.), *The Minutes of Edinburgh Trades Council, 1859 – 1873* (Edinburgh: Scottish History Society, 1968). edited example of a key source for Victorian trade unionism.

Parliamentary Papers. The official enquiries for which the period is justly famous are an indispensable historical source – for the attitudes of the investigators as well as for their findings! Major enquiries in the second half of the century included Royal Commissions on Trade Unions (1867), Friendly Societies

(1871 – 4), Housing (1884 – 5), and Labour (1892 – 4); all these and much else of relevance appear in the Irish University Press series of facsimile reprints of Parliamentary Papers.

Razell, P. E., and Wainwright, R. W. (eds), *The Victorian Working Class: Selections from Letters to the Morning Chronicle* (1973). Newspaper series (the 'letters' were in fact lengthy commissioned articles) first published 1849, describing social conditions in various parts of England and Wales; far more conventional in approach than Mayhew's articles on London (see next item), which they accompanied.

Thompson, E. P., and Yeo, E. (eds), *The Unknown Mayhew* (1971). Penetrating contemporary analysis of the growth of sweating; unusually among Victorian observers, Mayhew allows working people to speak for themselves and takes their own analysis of their situation seriously.

Wright, Thomas, *The Great Unwashed* (reprint 1970; first published 1868). Classic semi-autobiographical description of working-class life and attitudes from the point of view of skilled labour, first published under the pseudonym 'Journeyman Engineer'; like many contemporary accounts, this is part of the debate about the consequences of parliamentary reform (note date of publication).

SECTION II: HISTORICAL STUDIES

Note: the bibliographies published annually by the Society for the Study of Labour History in its *Bulletin* are an indispensable reference aid for current work.

Titles of journals are abbreviated as follows:

EcHR : *Economic History Review,* 2nd series
IRSH : *International Review of Social History*
SH : *Social History*

Alexander, S., '*Women's Work in Nineteenth-Century London*', in J. Mitchell and A. Oakley (eds), *Rights and Wrongs of Women* (Harmondsworth, 1976).

Allen, E., *et al.*, *The North-East Engineers' Strikes of 1871* (Newcastle-on-Tyne, 1971).

Anderson, M., *Family Structure in Nineteenth-Century Lancashire* (Cambridge, 1971).

Bailey, P., 'Will the Real Bill Banks Please Stand Up?', *Journal of*

70

Social History, 12 (1979). Questions over-simple interpretations of commitment to respectability.

Barnsby, G., 'The Standard of Living in the Black Country', *EcHR,* 24 (1971).

Bell, Donald H., 'Worker Culture and Worker Politics: the Experience of an Italian Town, 1880–1915', *SH,* vol. 3 (1978).

Best, G., *Mid-Victorian Britain 1851–1875* (1971).

Brown, M. Barratt, *After Imperialism* (revised edn, 1970). Of relevance to the economic context of working-class development.

Burgess, K., 'Technological Change and the 1852 Lock-out in the British Engineering Industry', *IRSH,* 14 (1969). Important study, quantifying the spread of new technologies and showing their relationship to industrial conflict.

——, 'Trade Union Policy and the 1852 Lock-out in the British Engineering Industry', *IRSH,* 17 (1972). Cf. Murphy [1978].

——, *The Origins of British Industrial Relations* (1975).

Cambridge Journal of Economics, 3 (1979). Contains several articles on the labour process in nineteenth-century industry.

Child, J., *Industrial Relations in the British Printing Industry* (1967).

Clegg, H. A., Fox, A., and Thompson, A. F., *A History of British Trade Unions Since 1889.* (Oxford, 1964).

Cole, G. D. H., 'Some Notes on British Trade Unions in the Third Quarter of the Nineteenth Century', reprinted in E. M. Carus-Wilson (ed.), *Essays in British Economic History,* vol. III (1962).

Crossick, G., *An Artisan Elite in Victorian Society: Kentish London, 1840–1880* (1978). An important local study, of wider significance.

——, (ed.), *The Lower Middle Class in Britain, 1870–1914* (1977). Essays on various aspects of this hitherto neglected social group, often assumed to be socially close to the labour aristocracy.

Cullen, M. J., 'The 1887 Survey of the London Working Class', *IRSH,* 20 (1975).

Cunningham, H., *The Volunteer Force* (1976).

Davidoff, L., 'Mastered for Life', *Journal of Social History,* 7 (1974). Relates domestic service to the subordination of women in society and the family.

Donajgrodzki, A. P. (ed.), *Social Control in Nineteenth-Century Britain* (1977).

Field, J., 'British Historians and the Concept of the Labour Aristocracy', *Radical History Review*, 19 (1978–9). Stimulating discussion of the value and limitations of different uses of the concept.

Foster, J., *Class Struggle and the Industrial Revolution* (1974). A controversial interpretation of the emergence of the labour aristocracy, based on a pioneering local study of Oldham; this important work continues to stimulate discussion: see especially Stedman Jones (1975).

Fraser, W. Hamish, *Trade Unions and Society: the Struggle for Acceptance, 1850–1880* (1974).

Gilding, B., *The Journeymen Coopers of East London* (History Workshop pamphlet, 1971). A detailed study of working practice and craft custom.

Gray, R. Q., *The Labour Aristocracy in Victorian Edinburgh* (Oxford, 1976). See comments in Field [1978–9], Moorhouse [1978], Morris [1977].

Gupta, P. S., *Imperialism and the British Labour Movement 1914–1964* (1975). See ch. 1 for discussion of the pre-First World War background.

Hanson, C. G., 'Craft Unions, Benefits and the Case for Trade Union Law Reform, 1867–1875', *EcHR*, 28 (1975). See also Thane [1976].

Harrison, R., *Before the Socialists: Studies in Labour and Politics, 1861–1881* (1965).

——, (ed.) *Independent Collier* (1978). A major contribution, this collection of essays challenges much received wisdom about the mining industry.

Hobsbawm, E. J., *Labouring Men* (1964a). Includes a well-known essay on the labour aristocracy, and other pioneering studies of the nineteenth-century working class.

——, 'The Nineteenth-Century London Labour Market', in R. Glass (ed.), *London: Aspects of Change* (1964b).

Hopkin, D., 'The Membership of the Independent Labour Party, 1904–1910: a Spatial and Occupational Analysis', *IRSH*, 20 (1975).

Hopkins, E., 'Small Town Aristocrats of Labour and their Standard of Living, 1840–1914', *EcHR*, 28 (1975). Study of glass-workers in Stourbridge; also looks comparatively at more depressed groups.

Hunt, E. H., *Regional Wage Variations in Britain, 1850–1914* (Oxford, 1973).

Jeffreys, J. B., *The Story of the Engineers* (1945). A model trade union history, places institutional development in its economic, industrial and social context.

Jeffreys, M., and Jeffreys, J. B., 'The Wages, Hours and Trade Customs of Skilled Engineers in 1861', *EcHR* 1st series, 17 (1947).

Jones, G. Stedman, *Outcast London* (Oxford, 1971). A major study of casual labour and sweating.

——, 'Working Class Culture and Working Class Politics in London, 1870–1900', *Journal of Social History*, 7 (1974).

——, 'Class Struggle and the Industrial Revolution', *New Left Review*, 90 (1975). Discussion of Foster [1974].

——, 'Class Expression versus Social Control: a Critique of Recent Trends in the Social History of Leisure', *History Workshop Journal*, 4 (1977).

Joyce, P., 'The Factory Politics of Lancashire in the Later Nineteenth Century', *Historical Journal*, 18 (1975).

Kingsford, P. W., *Victorian Railwaymen* (1970).

Lenin, V. I., *Imperialism: the Highest Stage of Capitalism*, in *Selected Works* (one vol. edn, Moscow, 1968; also available in numerous other edns). Contains Lenin's sketchy but influential comments on the labour aristocracy. Cf. Barratt Brown [1970].

Levitt, I., and Smout, T. C., *The State of the Scottish Working Class in 1843* (Edinburgh, 1979). See especially ch. 5-7.

Liddington, J., and Norris, J., *One Hand Tied Behind Us: the Rise of the Women's Suffrage Movement* (1978). Uses oral evidence to relate suffrage and trade union activity to industrial and family structure.

Lunn, K. (ed.), *Hosts, Immigrants and Minorities* (1980).

Marx, K., *Capital*, vol. I (Harmondsworth; Pelican edn, 1976). See chs 13–15 for Marx's analysis of different forms of production under capitalism.

Marx, K., and Engels, F., *On Britain* (1962). See especially Engels's 1892 preface to the *Condition of the Working Class*, and comments in letters.

Melling, J., 'Noncommissioned Officers: British Employers and their Supervisory Workers, 1880–1920', *SH*, vol. 5 (1980). A major contribution, exploring a hitherto neglected topic.

Moorhouse, H. F., 'The Marxist Theory of the Labour Aristocracy', *SH*, vol. 3 (1978). Stimulating critique of the concept: see also Reid [1978].

Morris, R. J., 'Bargaining with Hegemony', *Bulletin of the Society for the Study of Labour History*, 35 (1977). Review article discussing Gray [1976]; makes original points of great interest.

——, *Class and Class Consciousness in the Industrial Revolution, 1780–1850* (1979).

Moss, Bernard H., *The Origins of the French Labor Movement, 1830–1914: the Socialism of Skilled Workers* (Berkley and London, 1976). Suggests interesting similarities and comparisons with Britain; assumes existence of British labour aristocracy and argues there was no French equivalent.

Murphy, P. J., 'The Origins of the 1852 Lock-out in the British Engineering Industry Reconsidered', *IRSH*, 23 (1978). Criticises Jeffreys [1945] and Burgess [1972].

Musson, A. E., *British Trade Unions, 1800–1875* (1962).

Neale, R. S., 'The Standard of Living, 1780–1844: a Regional and Class Study', *EcHR*, 19 (1966). Of wider methodological importance.

Pelling, H., *Popular Politics and Society in Late Victorian Britain* (1968). Includes a critique of the labour aristocracy, and essays on other relevant themes.

Pollard, S., *History of Labour in Sheffield* (1959).

——, 'Nineteenth-Century Cooperation: from Community-Building to Shopkeeping', in A. Briggs and J. Saville (eds), *Essays in Labour History* (1960).

Porter, J. H., 'Wages Bargaining under Conciliation Agreements, 1860–1914', *EcHR*, 23 (1970).

Price, R., 'The Working Men's Club Movement and Victorian Social Reform Ideology', *Victorian Studies*, 15 (1971).

——, *An Imperial War and the British Working Class* (1972).

——, 'The Other Face of Respectability: Violence in the Manchester Brickmaking Trade, 1859–1870', *Past and Present*, 66 (1975).

Prothero, I. J., 'London Chartism and the Trades', *EcHR*, 24 (1971).

Reid, A., 'Politics and Economics in the Formation of the British Working Class: a Response to H. F. Moorhouse', *SH*, vol. 3 (1978).

Reid, D. A., 'The Decline of Saint Monday, 1766–1876', *Past and Present*, 71 (1976).

Roberts, E., 'Working-Class Standards of Living in Barrow and Lancaster, 1890–1914', *EcHR*, 30 (1977). Uses oral evidence.

Roberts, R., *The Classic Slum* (Manchester, 1971).

Robertson, P. L., 'Technical Education in the British Ship-building and Marine Engineering Industry, 1863–1914', *EcHR*, 27 (1974).

—, 'Demarcation Disputes in British Shipbuilding before 1914', *IRSH*, 20 (1975).

Samuel, R., 'The Workshop of the World: Steam Power and Hand Technology in Mid-Victorian Britain', *History Workshop Journal*, 3 (1977).

Schmiechen, J. A., 'State Reform and the Local Economy: an Aspect of Industrialisation in Late Victorian and Edwardian London', *EcHR*, 28 (1975). Shows how attempts to control out-work in some districts led to its intensification in others.

Scott, Joan, *The Glass Workers of Carmaux* (Cambridge, Mass., 1974). Excellent local and occupational study of French skilled labour.

Semmel, B., *Imperialism and Social Reform* (1960).

Shepherd, M. A., 'The Origins and Incidence of the Term "Labour Aristocracy"', *Bulletin of Society for the Study of Labour History*, 37 (1978). See also comment by Melling, ibid. (Autumn 1979).

Slaven, A., 'Earnings and Productivity in the Scottish Coal-mining Industry during the Nineteenth Century', in P. L. Payne (ed,), *Studies in Scottish Business History* (1967).

Storch, R. D., 'The Plague of Blue Locusts', *IRSH*, 20 (1975).

Summers, A., 'Militarism in Britain before the Great War', *History Workshop Journal*, 2 (1976).

Taylor, S., 'The Effect of Marriage on Job Possibilities for Women and the Ideology of the Home: Nottingham, 1890–1930', *Oral History*, 5 (1977).

Thane, P., 'Craft Unions, Welfare Benefits and the Case for Trade Union Reform', *EcHR*, 29 (1976). Rejoinder to Hanson [1975].

Tholfsen, T., *Working-Class Radicalism in Mid-Victorian England* (1976). Emphasises continuities of earlier popular radicalism and middle-class Liberalism.

Thompson, E. P., 'The Peculiarities of the English', reprinted in *The Poverty of Theory and Other Essays* (1978). Interpretative essay taking a broad sweep of English social history; includes perceptive comments on the character of the labour movement.

Treble, J. H., 'The Seasonal Demand for Labour in Glasgow, 1890–1914', *SH*, vol. 3 (1978).

Turner, H. A., *Trade Union Growth, Structure and Policy: a Study of the Cotton Unions* (1962). Explores problems of 'closed' or 'open' forms of organisation; of great relevance to concepts of labour aristocracy.

Vincent, J. R., *The Formation of the Liberal Party* (1966). Emphasises popular demands for participation and social recognition as part of the dynamic of Liberalism.

Webb, S., and Webb, B., *The History of British Trade Unions* (revised edn, 1920). Classic study that deservedly remains influential; for criticisms see Cole [1962] and Musson [1962].

Yeo, S., *Religion and Voluntary Organisations in Crisis* (1976). Explores the theme of civic participation in a number of contexts in Reading.

Index